An Analysis of

Marcus Aurelius's

Meditations

James Orr

LONDON AND NEW YORK

Published by Macat International Ltd
24:13 Coda Centre, 189 Munster Road, London SW6 6AW.

Distributed exclusively by Routledge
2 Park Square, Milton Park, Abingdon, Oxon OX14 4RN
605 Third Avenue, New York, NY 10017

Routledge is an imprint of the Taylor & Francis Group, an informa business

Copyright © 2017 by Macat International Ltd
Macat International has asserted its right under the Copyright, Designs and Patents Act
1988 to be identified as the copyright holder of this work.

www.macat.com
info@macat.com

Cataloguing in Publication Data
A catalogue record for this book is available from the British Library.
Cover illustration: Capucine Deslouis

ISBN 978-1-912303-08-3 (hardback)
ISBN 978-1-912128-39-6 (paperback)
ISBN 978-1-912281-96-1 (e-book)

CONTENTS

THE MACAT LIBRARY

The Macat Library is a series of unique academic explorations of seminal works in the humanities and social sciences – books and papers that have had a significant and widely recognised impact on their disciplines. It has been created to serve as much more than just a summary of what lies between the covers of a great book. It illuminates and explores the influences on, ideas of, and impact of that book. Our goal is to offer a learning resource that encourages critical thinking and fosters a better, deeper understanding of important ideas.

Each publication is divided into three Sections: Influences, Ideas, and Impact. Each Section has four Modules. These explore every important facet of the work, and the responses to it.

This Section-Module structure makes a Macat Library book easy to use, but it has another important feature. Because each Macat book is written to the same format, it is possible (and encouraged!) to cross-reference multiple Macat books along the same lines of inquiry or research. This allows the reader to open up interesting interdisciplinary pathways.

To further aid your reading, lists of glossary terms and people mentioned are included at the end of this book (these are indicated by an asterisk [*] throughout) – as well as a list of works cited.

Macat has worked with the University of Cambridge to identify the elements of critical thinking and understand the ways in which six different skills combine to enable effective thinking.
Three allow us to fully understand a problem; three more give us the tools to solve it. Together, these six skills make up the **PACIER** model of critical thinking. They are:

ANALYSIS – understanding how an argument is built
EVALUATION – exploring the strengths and weaknesses of an argument
INTERPRETATION – understanding issues of meaning

CREATIVE THINKING – coming up with new ideas and fresh connections
PROBLEM-SOLVING – producing strong solutions
REASONING – creating strong arguments

To find out more, visit **WWW.MACAT.COM.**

CRITICAL THINKING AND *MEDITATIONS*

Primary critical thinking skill: PROBLEM-SOLVING
Secondary critical thinking skill: CREATIVE THINKING

Despite being written between 170 and 180, Marcus Aurelius' *Meditations* often resonates with modern readers because of its remarkable resemblance to a self-help book. Written as a series of personal notes in the last decade of his reign as Roman emperor, the meditations were never intended for circulation. But they remain today among the classics of stoic philosophy – and as exquisite examples of problem-solving.

Meditations sees a great leader engaged in solving one of the central problems of all philosophy: how to live a good life. Marcus Aurelius is quick to ask questions and generate solutions, all of which lead him to a greater understanding of what a good life really is. He makes the decision that philosophy is an important tool we can use every day to help us understand and deal with the world. The best way to get to the bottom of a problem, he records, is to analyze its different aspects with care – this will help to 'dissolve' the issue. To keep our minds well balanced, it is vital to keep our desire for the material and the sensual in check to avoid falling prey to negative behaviors like jealousy, quarrelling and indulgence. Philosophy, the *Meditations* show, can also help us to understand other people's problems and difficulties – acting as a continual spur to the consideration and resolution of problems, wherever they arise.

ABOUT THE AUTHOR OF THE ORIGINAL WORK

Known both as one of Rome's "Five Good Emperors" and as an important philosopher, **Marcus Aurelius** was born in 121 C.E. and was emperor of Rome from 161 C.E. until 180 C.E., at first in partnership with Lucius Verus until the latter's death in 169 C.E. The empire was at its height, and Marcus—disciplined, conscientious, self-aware—was arguably the most powerful man in the world. Yet despite the might of Rome, Marcus had to spend much of his reign pacifying Germanic tribes in the Balkans and southern Germany, where he died aged 58 in 180 C.E. It is likely that he composed his famous personal writings, *Meditations*, during these campaigns.

ABOUT THE AUTHOR OF THE ANALYSIS

Dr James Orr holds a DPhil in the philosophy of religion from the University of Cambridge. He is currently the McDonald Postdoctoral Fellow in Theology, Ethics, and Public Life at Christ Church College, Oxford.

ABOUT MACAT

GREAT WORKS FOR CRITICAL THINKING

Macat is focused on making the ideas of the world's great thinkers accessible and comprehensible to everybody, everywhere, in ways that promote the development of enhanced critical thinking skills.

It works with leading academics from the world's top universities to produce new analyses that focus on the ideas and the impact of the most influential works ever written across a wide variety of academic disciplines. Each of the works that sit at the heart of its growing library is an enduring example of great thinking. But by setting them in context – and looking at the influences that shaped their authors, as well as the responses they provoked – Macat encourages readers to look at these classics and game-changers with fresh eyes. Readers learn to think, engage and challenge their ideas, rather than simply accepting them.

'Macat offers an amazing first-of-its-kind tool for interdisciplinary learning and research. Its focus on works that transformed their disciplines and its rigorous approach, drawing on the world's leading experts and educational institutions, opens up a world-class education to anyone.'

Andreas Schleicher
Director for Education and Skills, Organisation for Economic Co-operation and Development

'Macat is taking on some of the major challenges in university education … They have drawn together a strong team of active academics who are producing teaching materials that are novel in the breadth of their approach.'

Prof Lord Broers,
former Vice-Chancellor of the University of Cambridge

'The Macat vision is exceptionally exciting. It focuses upon new modes of learning which analyse and explain seminal texts which have profoundly influenced world thinking and so social and economic development. It promotes the kind of critical thinking which is essential for any society and economy. This is the learning of the future.'

Rt Hon Charles Clarke, former UK Secretary of State for Education

'The Macat analyses provide immediate access to the critical conversation surrounding the books that have shaped their respective discipline, which will make them an invaluable resource to all of those, students and teachers, working in the field.'

Professor William Tronzo, University of California at San Diego

WAYS IN TO THE TEXT

KEY POINTS

- Marcus Aurelius (121–180 c.e.) ruled as emperor of Rome between 161 c.e. and his death, following lengthy military campaigns against Germanic tribes.
- *Meditations* focuses on a wide range of philosophical questions that arise in everyday life.
- Although resistant to any obvious literary classification, *Meditations* is better understood as a philosophical manual for confronting everyday problems than as a systematic work of theoretical philosophy.

Who Was Marcus Aurelius?

Marcus Aurelius, the author of *Meditations*, was the adopted son of the emperor of Rome, Antoninus Pius,* the founder of the Antonine dynasty, who ruled from 138 to 161 c.e. At the death of Antoninus, Marcus succeeded him, ruling until 180 c.e. His legacy is mixed as a military commander and political ruler, and his lack of caution over the succession of his son Commodus* had severe consequences for the stability of the Roman Empire* in the late second century. Nevertheless, he is famously included in the list of "Five Good Emperors" proposed in 1503 by the Italian Renaissance* political theorist Niccolò Machiavelli,* together with Nerva,* Trajan,* Hadrian,* and his predecessor Antoninus Pius.

His most famous achievement, however, outranks the achievements of many other emperors: his composition, in Greek, of the reflections that have come to be known as *Meditations*. It seems that he wrote the small volume in the last decade of his life (between around 170 C.E. and 180 C.E.). This was a period of intense military activity for Marcus Aurelius, who was leading punishing campaigns against tribes in Germany and around the central European river Danube. Yet the demanding circumstances in which Marcus wrote his personal reflections are seen by him as challenges to be overcome, following the philosophical principles and practices of the Stoic* tradition, emphasizing the pursuit of reason and indifference to physical hardship. His work has exercised more influence over the Western intellectual tradition than that of any other Roman emperor. He is commonly regarded as an outstanding example of someone who integrated deep and careful reflection about life with the practical day-to-day demands of political leadership.

What Does *Meditations* Say?

The English title of the work is, in fact, an attempt to render the Greek phrase pronounced *ta eis heauton* (literally "things that relate to oneself"). The small book was intended, therefore, as Marcus's reflections on life—reflections profoundly shaped by the philosophy of Stoicism, especially as it is set out in the writings of the Greek-born philosopher Epictetus* and the Roman philosopher Seneca.* With Platonism* (the school of philosophy founded by the Greek philosopher Plato*), Aristotelianism* (the school founded by Plato's student Aristotle*), and Epicureanism* (the school founded by the Greek philosopher Epicurus*), Stoicism was one of the four principal schools of Greco-Roman philosophy. Most scholars agree, however, that *Meditations* resists classification into any ancient literary genre: the text neither qualifies as a biography, diary, formal philosophical discourse, nor instructive work. In many respects the work bears a closer resemblance to more recent literary genres that focus on the pursuit of personal wisdom, self-knowledge, and the nature of the interior life.

If *Meditations* is not a work that aims to convey a single overarching message, this is partly because its philosophical reflections are closely linked to practical solutions to problems in everyday life. It is also a consequence of the fact that there is no evidence that Marcus intended the collection to be a literary work—or indeed to be read by anyone but himself. Nevertheless, there are certainly identifiable themes in the work, chiefly a series of straightforward methods to apply in practical ethics (questions of how morality is applied in everyday action). Moreover, the work is underpinned by the basic Stoic conviction that "a virtuous life is a happy life," where emotions and desires are significantly dependent on the beliefs and understanding that people have about the world, and that humans possess an inbuilt "moral sympathy" for other humans, regardless of social or ethnic differences.

These are all thoughts that spring up in different corners of the Western philosophical tradition. For instance, the tight equation of virtue and happiness is central to an ethical theory known as "eudaimonism,"* an approach formulated as early as the fifth and fourth centuries B.C.E. by Plato and developed with great sophistication by Aristotle. Similarly, the notion that there is a moral sentiment common to all human beings is one that was advanced influentially in the eighteenth century by the great Scottish Enlightenment* philosophers Adam Smith* and David Hume.* Although Stoicism is generally seen by many as opposed to Epicureanism, the text aims to instill in its reader the need to cultivate a state of what Epicurus labeled *ataraxia**—a Greek term best translated as a state of "freedom from worldly worry."

Meditations is also notable for the way Marcus argues for a viewpoint that enables us to escape our particular place in the affairs of the world, and in particular the conflicts and crises that our emotional attachments to the world can bring with them. The philosophically reflective stance that he recommends also equips us with a perspective that allows us to give appropriate weight to different features of our daily experience by striking a balance between our emotional and our cognitive responses to the world.

Why Does *Meditations* Matter?

Meditations has had a significant influence on many important historical figures in the four centuries or so since it became widely known (it was unavailable in print until 1558). It is also unique in providing an insight into the sophisticated philosophical mind of a historical figure who played an enormously significant political role during the era in which he lived. Indeed, there are no other examples from antiquity of a truly important ruler's personal reflections, insights, and self-reflections having survived for nearly two millennia. It is also a text that has a great deal of contemporary relevance, not least because it takes philosophy to be first and foremost a practical matter. In this, Marcus anticipated to some extent the way in which the Austrian British philosopher Ludwig Wittgenstein,* one of the twentieth century's greatest thinkers, attempted to overturn the overly theoretical character of philosophy. Philosophy, claimed Wittgenstein, should function as a form of intellectual therapy: in particular, it should help us to resolve anxieties generated by the fact that humans are cognitively limited and morally fragile beings.

Meditations is hailed by many historians of ideas such as the French scholars Pierre Hadot* and Michel Foucault* as a text that treats philosophy as a vital tool for conduct in daily life, and not as the pursuit of an abstract system of theoretical speculation. A similar approach to philosophy can be found in the American philosopher Richard Rorty's* influential attack on what he perceived to be the excessively abstract and theoretical character of Anglo-American philosophy.[1]

Much of the success of *Meditations* in contemporary culture can be attributed to its success as an accessible, practical guide to life that does not require the degree of commitment that grander philosophical or theological* belief-systems demand of their followers. The increasing popular appetite for so-called "self-help" literature in today's world is an important factor in accounting for the popularity of the book today and its enduring appeal. *Meditations* is a work that anticipates by nearly two thousand years the kind of philosophy put forward today on how to deal with the practical challenges and anxieties of everyday life. It also echoes very neatly the fashion in twenty-first century literature and culture for introspective analyses of a life lived in a philosophically reflective way.

NOTES

1   Richard Rorty, *Philosophy and the Mirror of Nature* (Princeton, NJ: Princeton University Press, 1979).

SECTION 1
INFLUENCES

MODULE 1
THE AUTHOR AND THE
HISTORICAL CONTEXT

KEY POINTS

- *Meditations* takes a resolutely practical approach to philosophical challenges.

- The uniqueness of *Meditations* lies in the insight it gives us into the mind of a pivotal figure in the history of the ancient world.

- Greek philosophy and literature played an important part in Marcus's intellectual formation.

Why Read This Text?

Today, Marcus Aurelius's *Meditations* (written circa 170–180 C.E.) is one of the most widely read works of ancient literature. Among the many reasons to explain this interest is its careful, reflective stance on the dilemmas and difficulties that confront us all in everyday life. Unlike much of current academic philosophy in the English-speaking world, it does not focus on devising an abstract system of thought or on developing a theory of reality consistent with the increasing complexity of modern science. Rather, its central aim is to take seriously the therapeutic power of attaining philosophical wisdom and applying it to the concerns that affect almost every human being: mortality, temptation, anxiety, and so on.

In other words, *Meditations* takes an unashamedly pragmatic approach. It offers a much more intelligible and accessible form of philosophy for those unfamiliar with the thought of the major philosophers in the last four centuries. However, the text is important,

> ❝ From his earliest moments [Marcus Aurelius] was the recipient and heir of immense wealth and privilege for, next to the obvious factor of wealth, kinship decided life chances in the Roman Empire. ❞
>
> Frank McLynn, *Marcus Aurelius: Warrior, Philosopher, Emperor*

too, because it provides a uniquely detailed insight into the mind of a key figure in the ancient world, the Roman emperor himself, who necessarily had to tackle a vast array of complex challenges— whether political, military, or economic. There is, quite simply, no other work from antiquity that resembles *Meditations*.

Author's Life

Marcus was born on April 26, 121 C.E. in the town of Ucubi near Córdoba in the Roman province of Baetica in southern Spain. This was an administrative region that roughly overlaps with the Islamic* region of Andalucía founded after the conquest of the Iberian peninsula by the Umayyad Caliphate* in the eighth century C.E. The Roman Empire* was then at the peak of its dominance of the Mediterranean world. He was the favored offspring of a well-to-do family with important connections to the imperial household and, indeed, to the imperial family. Marcus was first noticed by the Emperor Hadrian* before he had reached the age of eight; Hadrian personally enrolled him in the Salii,* a priestly caste open to aristocratic young men, whose duties he exercised with great seriousness. He was also conspicuous at a young age for his high levels of intelligence and personal modesty. At 14, he was robed in the *toga virilis*, a garment given to Roman males to mark their coming-of-age; this led to a rapid ascent of the ladder of executive and administrative power. At the end of his reign, Hadrian was exhausted by the business of choosing a successor, and had been suffering for years from illnesses. When he died in 138 C.E., he was succeeded by Antoninus Pius,* with Marcus becoming leader of the knights of the equestrian order*—*princeps iuventutis* ("prince of youth"). As emperor of Rome, Antoninus exerted enormous influence over Marcus, eventually encouraging him to marry his daughter and thus become his heir.

When Antoninus died in March 161 C.E., Marcus succeeded him alongside a co-emperor, Lucius Verus,* in accordance with Hadrian's original wishes. The period of joint rule saw the beginnings of serious unrest not only in Parthia (a region now in north-eastern Iran), where a Roman legion was massacred, but also in Dalmatia (the main coastal region of modern-day Croatia) and Dardania (a province in the modern-day Balkans). Military campaigns kept both emperors occupied for much of their respective reigns.

In 169 C.E., Lucius died and Marcus became sole ruler of Rome. From then on, he was permanently engaged in fending off sporadic attacks by Germanic tribes in the northern part of the Roman Empire. At the same time, unrest arose in Cappadocia and in Bithynia (modern-day Turkey). Worn down by military responsibilities for which he had received very little training from his predecessor Antoninus, who had ruled an empire that remained largely at peace, Marcus died in Vindobona (modern-day Vienna) on March 17, 180 C.E. After his death, he was formally deified by the Roman state and his ashes were interred in the mausoleum of the Emperor Hadrian—the man who had done more than any other to ensure Marcus's rise to the summit of imperial power.

Author's Background

After the accession of Antoninus, Marcus's intellectual development continued at a rapid pace. He soon encountered the thought of the Greek philosopher Apollonius,* a follower of the rational, detached principles of the Stoic* school of philosophy. He was also taught rhetoric by a brilliant tutor, Fronto,* much of whose correspondence with Marcus has survived. Another significant influence on Marcus was Quintus Junius Rusticus,* a teacher responsible for introducing Marcus to Greek thought (and Stoic philosophy in particular). At one point Marcus made the remark that it was through Rusticus that he came to know the *Discourses* of Epictetus*—a work by the most influential exponent of Stoicism in the Roman world. Marcus was also brought up studying the work of the great Greek philosopher of change and flux, Heraclitus.*

Marcus's paternal grandfather had married Rupilia Faustina,* who was in the patrician class,* one of many levels in the fine-grained social hierarchy of ancient Rome. This crucial family connection to the aristocracy had the greatest impact on his life after, of course, the Emperor Hadrian himself. Marcus lost his father at the age of three in 124 C.E., but *Meditations* contains passages expressing deep gratitude for and awareness of his reputation as a statesman and as a person. At an early stage in his life, he was taught to read and write Greek; many aspects of the writings of the epic poet Homer* dominate Marcus's thought-world, further accounting for his lifelong cultivation of an austere, restrained way of life.

MODULE 2
ACADEMIC CONTEXT

KEY POINTS

- *Meditations* does not appear to have been intended for any audience other than the author himself.
- The Greek philosopher Epictetus,* a notable exponent of the philosophy of detachment and rationality known as Stoicism,* was the most crucial influence on Marcus's philosophical leanings.
- Marcus was also well versed in the writings of a wide range of Greek philosophers.

The Work in its Context

One of the most striking features of Marcus Aurelius's *Meditations* is that it is, in effect, a personal notebook that does not ever appear to have been intended to be read by anyone other than its author. It is a historical accident that the manuscript was preserved and passed on by someone in the imperial entourage, and was eventually rediscovered and published in 1558—though it is mentioned in texts from 364 C.E. and the ninth century.

The immediate biographical conditions in which *Meditations* was written gives its reader the unusual sense of getting to know the inner thoughts of an ancient historical figure who held a remarkable degree of power and influence. It is as if you are peering over the shoulder of someone composing a private diary. While the work is unique—there are no other examples of private writing like this that have survived from antiquity—it can also be understood as a response to the Stoic belief that the process of writing dispassionate descriptions of the challenges thrown up by life will, in itself, equip

> ❝ [Stoics] were ... aware ... that Epicureanism,
> Stoicism, Platonism,* and Aristotelianism* were
> merely the different and opposing forms of a single
> phenomenon: the philosophical style of life. Within
> the latter, there could be points held in common
> by several—or even all—of the schools, as Marcus
> states expressly. ❞
>
> Pierre Hadot, *The Inner Citadel: The Meditations of Marcus Aurelius*

the writer to overcome them.[1] In other words, the simple fact of
writing the book was a way of treating philosophy as a therapeutic
exercise to help tackle the difficulties of everyday life with greater
insight and confidence.

Overview of the Field

It is clear that behind the composition of *Meditations* was a
mind acutely aware of the writings of key ancient literary and
philosophical figures, in particular the poet Homer* and the
thinkers Heraclitus* and Seneca.* But it is the first and second
century C.E. Greek Stoic philosopher Epictetus who counts as the
major intellectual influence on *Meditations*. Epictetus died at about
the time that Marcus received the *toga virilis* marking his coming-
of-age as a Roman citizen. A slave from Phrygia (in modern-day
Turkey), Epictetus lived and taught in Rome for most of his life.
His lectures, which came to be known as *Discourses*, were written
down by his pupil Arrian.* The overarching emphasis of Epictetus's
teaching in *Discourses* was that philosophy should affect a person's
entire way of life and not be confined to theoretical domains. As
a Stoic, Epictetus was a fatalist*—that is, someone who believed
reality was ultimately driven by forces that human beings could
not influence. But Stoics departed from the Epicureans* in the

belief that history is determined by an underlying universal rational principle or *logos*.

Academic Influences

It is clear that Marcus shapes *Meditations* around some of the teachings Epictetus recommends to those wishing to pursue a philosophical way of life. The work also shows signs of engagement with a wide range of other figures. It is known that although Marcus was a Stoic, he appreciated the work of Epicurus,* the founder of the major rival to Stoic thought, Epicureanism. He also includes many references to, and quotations from, the philosophers Heraclitus,* Plato,* Democritus,* and Chrysippus,* the third head of the Stoic school in Athens, often known as its "second founder" after Zeno of Citium.* It was Chrysippus who systematized a definite account of Stoic philosophy, and it is to his work that Stoic philosophy owed its legacy and longevity.

Finally, the ideas of Heraclitus, one of the most important pre-Socratic philosophers (the philosophers who came before the extremely influential Greek thinker Socrates*), play a crucial role in the way Marcus formulates several of his positions in *Meditations*. From the surviving fragments of his work, Heraclitus emphasized change as the most fundamental feature of reality: everything that exists is in a permanent state of flux and instability. This emphasis on the fleeting nature of our desires and the objects of our desires is central to Marcus's repeated advice to himself that he should not become attached to the temporary lure of luxury and power.

NOTES

1   Epictetus, *The Discourses of Epictetus*, trans. Robin Hard (London: Everyman, 1995), I.1.21–5.

MODULE 3
THE PROBLEM

KEY POINTS

- Marcus Aurelius places supreme importance on the mind as the faculty that should direct and govern behavior.

- In *Meditations*, Marcus draws a distinction between mind and body that owes more to the philosophy of Platonism* than his own Stoic* background.

- *Meditations* has influenced people of all kinds in the modern world.

Core Question

Among the practical questions Marcus Aurelius addresses in *Meditations* are:

- how to maintain an even temper when confronted with good fortune or tragedy in your life
- how to diffuse conflict with other people by seeing them as part of a common human family
- how to deal with the onset of physical sickness or psychological illness.

Although Marcus did not intend to resolve any of philosophy's grand theoretical questions, it is still possible to isolate one or two central themes in *Meditations* that link to many other questions.

One of the work's most distinctive features is the method that Marcus recommends for a life that engages wisely and reflectively with the challenges of everyday life. One of the main methods is to address a difficult topic by breaking it down into simpler parts.

❝ Marcus Aurelius's *Meditations* ... are not the spontaneous outpourings of a soul that wants to express its thoughts immediately, but rather an exercise, accomplished in accordance with definite rules. [They] presuppose an existing canvas, upon which the philosopher-emperor could only embroider. **❞**

Pierre Hadot, *The Inner Citadel: The* Meditations *of Marcus Aurelius*

The Greek word for "dividing up" or "dissolving" supplies the root for the English word "analyze." It is a style of careful, scrutinizing reflection on philosophical problems. One core idea is that it is the mind that is the "governing part" and "animating principle" of the self, rather than the flesh;[1] those who use the mind to govern the self are more likely to resist the trivial attractions of material concerns and sensory delight.

The Participants

Marcus engages himself in a debate in which the principal participants are the philosopher Epictetus* and the earlier thinker Plato.*

The emphasis Marcus places on the mind as the proper "directing" center of the self suggests a tension with traditional Stoic thought on the question of the relationship between the soul and the body. Like Epicureanism,* Stoicism was a materialist* philosophy. In other words, it maintained that nothing exists over and above material reality and (perhaps) the forces that animate matter. In elevating the mind over bodily desires, Marcus seems to depart from Stoicism's materialist view of the person, which denied the existence of immaterial minds.

Marcus appears instead to adopt an account of the mind and body more in keeping with the "dualist"* position of Plato, who, as made clear in dialogues such as *Phaedo* and *Meno*, is often interpreted as introducing a clear distinction between the soul (or mind) and the body as its disposable vehicle. This would suggest that Marcus takes a world-denying stance toward the material goods of the practical life, as some have accused Plato of doing, and as was characteristic of one or two other philosophical schools.

Other figures that qualify as participants in the work are the teachers whom Marcus thanks in the opening book, in particular Fronto* and Rusticus;* it is clear that Marcus sees himself as owing each a lasting debt for his intellectual development, even if he had departed from the teaching of Fronto in particular by the time he came to compose *Meditations*.

The Contemporary Debate

One of the most striking features of *Meditations* is Marcus's relative lack of interest in placing its themes and ideas within an intellectual tradition. Although it is clear that Marcus's outlook and core convictions are profoundly shaped by a systematic and sophisticated training in Stoic philosophy—particularly the extensive influence of Epictetus's *Discourses*—he does not really try to explain or evaluate any of its distinctive doctrines.

Although Marcus explicitly expresses intellectual debts to teachers such as Fronto and Rusticus, it is very difficult to trace the actual extent of his intellectual engagement with their views. Moreover, he very rarely (if at all) expresses a philosophical view in a way that implies he is attempting to distinguish it from views articulated by those who came before him. The originality of *Meditations* is not in the novelty of its philosophical contributions to the Stoic tradition, but rather in the skill and simplicity with which it formulates Stoicism's central beliefs as tools with which to gain control of one's character, to cultivate virtues (such as courage, wisdom, justice, and temperance) and to withstand otherwise destabilizing changes of fortune.

NOTES

1   Marcus Aurelius, *Meditations: With Selected Correspondence*, trans. Robin Hard (Oxford: Oxford University Press, 2011), 2.2, 5.26, 5.33, 12.3.

MODULE 4
THE AUTHOR'S CONTRIBUTION

KEY POINTS

- A central aim of *Meditations* is to focus its reader's attention on the transience of human experience.

- The unusual style of *Meditations* has parallels with much later texts such as the Meditations and Pensées of, respectively, the seventeenth-century French philosophers René Descartes* and Blaise Pascal.*

- *Meditations* simultaneously represents the culmination of classical Stoic* philosophy and can be seen as the last book in the catalogue of significant texts in the Stoic philosophical tradition.

Author's Aims

One of Marcus Aurelius's central aims when writing *Meditations* was to bring out the fleetingness of mortal existence. Influenced by the sixth century B.C.E. philosopher Heraclitus,* he dwells a great deal on notions of change, impermanence, and flux. On several occasions he compares the nature of change over time, for instance, to a roaring river that sweeps everything before it.[1] The idea is that nothing in reality is immune to ongoing, dynamic processes. This includes the possession of political power, the trappings of wealth and status, and the objects of our sensual pleasures and the great philosophical minds who shaped Marcus's thought: at one point he laments that the passing of time carried off Chrysippus,* perhaps the greatest thinker of the Stoic school in its early period, and also Epictetus,* the most influential Stoic author in the Roman Empire.* Nothing, in other words, is permanent.

❝ [For] Marcus Aurelius, philosophy was, above all, a way of life. This is why the *Meditations* strive, by means of an ever-renewed effort, to describe this way of life and to sketch the model that one must have constantly in view: that of the ideal good man. ❞

Pierre Hadot, *The Inner Citadel: The* Meditations *of Marcus Aurelius*

His goal in *Meditations* was to teach himself that it is through grasping this central idea that people can resist the many difficulties we suffer in our responses to ordinary day-to-day setbacks by applying the traditional Stoic dictum of "living according to virtue" or "living according to nature." The person who is aware of the ceaseless instability in the world is better equipped to develop a sense of acceptance of misfortune and so to remain calm in the face of irrational and intemperate emotional behavior.

Approach

The approach Marcus adopts in *Meditations* is unlike almost any other surviving ancient text. It is comparable in some ways to that of the seventeenth century philosophers René Descartes (in his own *Meditations*) and Blaise Pascal (in his *Pensées,* "Thoughts"), or the writer of the Book of Proverbs in the Old Testament: a loose collection of sequenced reflections, but without any of the formal or structural features you would expect to find in a philosophical work. It can strike the reader as loose and vague: there is no obvious thematic structure to the work, nor does it attempt to take on one or more complex questions in anything like a systematic manner. For many readers it is precisely the formlessness of *Meditations*, its resistance to any obvious literary classification, that commends it. It also applies the central commands of its teaching, namely the importance of applying oneself practically to problems with a philosophically balanced and partly detached approach. So the principal approach of the work is spiritual and intellectual formation, developing a set of detailed guidelines for an ethically satisfying and worthwhile life, with a repeated focus on the fleeting nature of human life. Another key approach is the need to maintain a proper perspective on the unfolding of physical and historical processes, and to learn to adopt a measured and temperate way of life that avoids placing undue importance on the meaningless fortunes and misfortunes that affect us individually.

Contribution in Context

Meditations takes its place alongside a handful of other writings in the catalogue of significant texts of Stoic philosophy. Indeed the work is the conclusion and culmination of Stoic writings that began with Chrysippus, Seneca,* the Roman thinker Musonius Rufus,* and, of course, his student Epictetus. It is clear that Marcus did not intend *Meditations* to be a formal contribution to Stoic philosophy as in the more systematic approach taken by figures such as Chrysippus. It is also widely agreed by scholars that he never intended the text to be read by anyone other than himself; as a result, it was not circulated till many years after his death and never had the impact on the development of Stoic philosophy in his own day that it might otherwise have done. Nevertheless, it remains perfectly legitimate to consider his contribution as the product of a mind steeped for many decades in Stoic teachings, practices, and writings.

It is for this reason that *Meditations* remains one of the most compact and readily understood accounts of Stoic philosophy to have survived from antiquity. The text has also made a significant contribution to today's fashion for works that offer advice on how to apply the mind to improving our emotional and mental habits, and thereby improving our moral conduct and the quality of our lives.

NOTES

1   See Marcus Aurelius, *Meditations: With Selected Correspondence*, trans. Robin Hard (Oxford: Oxford University Press, 2011), 4.43.

SECTION 2
IDEAS

MODULE 5
MAIN IDEAS

KEY POINTS

- *Meditations* returns again and again to the idea that philosophy should provide a practical guide to the challenges and changes of everyday life.

- A central idea of the text—and of Stoicism* more generally—is the universal moral worth of every human being.

- The fact that *Meditations* is written in Greek and not, as you might expect, in Marcus's native Latin, reveals the legacy of Greek thought on his philosophical outlook.

Key Themes

The principal themes of Marcus Aurelius's *Meditations* are as follows:

- the practice of philosophy as a way of life, much as some contemporary religious people think of their faith as a way of life rather than as a set of doctrinal principles, or prescribed teachings
- the transience and ceaseless change of reality
- the importance of "dissolving" through analysis the different components of a problem
- the task of developing a well-balanced mind that "governs" the self, and keeps in check its desires and wants for the material and sensual aspects of the world.

While these different strands are woven together in a number of ways, they are not set out as parts of the structure of the work, and

> **" Soon, you will have forgotten everything. Soon, everybody will have forgotten you! "**
>
> Marcus Aurelius, *Meditations*

simply emerge at several points as guiding threads and focal points of Marcus's philosophical thoughts. A recurring message of the work is the therapeutic power of reflecting in a careful and philosophically informed way on the vicissitudes (unwelcome changes) of mortal existence. The work encourages its readers to uncover the irrational grounds for so much of our emotional and mental behavior—petty jealousies, angry quarrels, and excessive consumption. By ensuring that the mind remains the governing center of the subject, these behavioral habits are uprooted as the mind analyzes and uncovers their causes in some false understanding of reality, such as the belief that material goods can provide eternal satisfaction. Our behavior toward others should be shaped by the Stoic philosophical stance sometimes known as cosmopolitanism*—that is, the idea that all human beings are "citizens" (*politai*) of the "world" (*cosmos*), belonging to a single universal family. It is to these core ideas that *Meditations* returns again and again.

Exploring the Ideas

At the heart of *Meditations*—and the Stoic philosophy of human nature more generally—is the thought that human beings have the capacity to reason and that, through reasoning, we can discipline the passions that drive the behavior of other animals. Marcus places great emphasis on the idea that the power of rationality is an almost-divine spark that can shape and guide our outlook and behavior—provided we take pains to exercise our capacity to reason. Our reasoning faculties are especially important for developing a clear-eyed recognition of the proper place of the individual in the grand unfolding of time and of the deep connections between human beings. Indeed, the idea that all human beings possess an intrinsic value comes to full fruition in the Stoic doctrine of cosmopolitanism, an idea with a rich pedigree in contemporary ethical and political philosophy. However, the belief that every human being is a being of value was not common in the ancient world. Indeed it seems the Stoics were among the first philosophers to conceive of all human beings as possessing moral worth (though this is also a stance associated with the thought and practice of early Christianity*).

Another theme recurring throughout *Meditations* that repays exploration is that of the relationship between a whole and its parts. The text has us understand that it is the task of the philosophically-attuned individual to evaluate every aspect of experience in terms of the specific function each of these parts contributes to the flourishing of the whole;[1] similarly, the individual soul is harmoniously integrated, as one part among many, within a comprehensive cosmic whole. This notion of general interconnectedness also underpins the Stoic theory of value that Marcus expresses at different points in *Meditations*, according to which the true value of an object that initially appears valueless emerges more clearly once it is assigned its proper place in the overarching structure of the cosmos.[2]

Language and Expression

Although it was not his native tongue, Marcus learnt to read and write Greek from a young age. Such was the influence of Greek poets and philosophers on his intellectual development that it is no surprise to find that *Meditations* is composed in Greek. While the style of Marcus's prose is sometimes obscure and awkward, on the whole his writing demonstrates a refreshing simplicity and directness. It is a testament to the depth of Greek influence on *Meditations* that it uses the same language as the greatest advocates of the Stoic way of life. Marcus's prose style is relaxed and full of vivid images and thought-provoking examples. His writing is not overly didactic (firmly instructive) in the way it sets out its philosophical positions and practical recommendations. He avoids lofty or flowery rhetoric and concentrates his thoughts into compact Greek sentences. On occasions the text reads fluently and easily, and on the whole avoids the abstract terms common to more systematic philosophical works. Marcus avoids the complex or technical jargon often employed in Stoic philosophy and almost always uses simple, familiar language; he often expresses himself with brief, arresting commands and pithy quotations such as "Do nothing randomly!"[3] Although *Meditations* often refers to events in its author's lifetime, they do not do so in much detail: the work is by no means a diary of Marcus's continuing attempts to apply the philosophy he prescribes.

NOTES

1   Marcus Aurelius, *Meditations: With Selected Correspondence*, trans. Robin Hard (Oxford: Oxford University Press, 2011), 6.45.

2   Marcus, *Meditations*, 3.2.

3   Marcus, *Meditations*, 2.17.

MODULE 6
SECONDARY IDEAS

KEY POINTS

- Marcus draws on the thought of the ancient Greek philosopher Plato* to argue that the well-being of the individual is organically connected to the well-being of the community.

- Marcus returns again and again to the claim that the mind and emotions of a person must be trained to confront the challenges of everyday life.

- Marcus's commitment to the deterministic* view that human action has no role to play in historical change (specifically the Stoic* doctrine of fatalism,* according to which history is nothing but the unfolding of fate) is not obviously compatible with the idea that human beings are free to prepare themselves intellectually and spiritually to face life's challenges.

Other Ideas

Many of the secondary ideas in Marcus Aurelius's *Meditations* arise from the principle that human beings should act in harmony with the characteristics with which nature (*phusis*) endows them. For Marcus, human behavior was only fitting or appropriate when people pursue ends consistent with nature; good actions, in other words, could only come from those who were in possession of a balanced, wise, and stable psychological outlook—and it follows that people should concentrate only on the challenge of acting justly and cultivating the place in the world that has been allotted to them.[1]

"Acting justly" is defined in terms of behavior geared toward the

> ❝ Be careful of becoming 'caesarized' … Keep
> yourself simple, good, pure, grave, natural, a
> friend of justice. Revere the gods, be benevolent,
> affectionate, and firm in accomplishing your duties.
> Fight in order to remain as philosophy has wished
> you to be. ❞
>
> Marcus Aurelius, *Meditations*

flourishing of the life of the community. This is an idea that will have
been familiar to ancient readers, since the link between individual
morality and political stability is a central theme of Plato's* most
famous dialogue, *Republic*.[2] However, there is a crucial distinction
between Marcus's ideas and the Platonic* model: Marcus interprets
the term "community" to mean the universal community of all
humanity, an idea drawn from Stoic philosophy. Human beings must
therefore ensure that reasoning should direct our emotions, desires,
and impulses toward communal action.[3] Marcus seems to have been
convinced that there is an actual faculty or instinct that binds humans
together as a species.[4] The good of the individual and the good of the
community are treated as one and the same aim for a life of justice.[5]

Exploring the Ideas

The ways in which *Meditations* tackles the question of how to
reconcile individual morality and political justice suggests that Marcus
disagreed with Plato on the role and obligations of the citizen. Unlike
Plato, Marcus believes that there will often be occasions in life where
the moral end of an individual might conflict with the moral aims of
a political community. Though Marcus underlines more than Plato
the notion that each individual has a functional role in the social
structure of his or her political community, he nevertheless denies the
Platonic idea of the equivalence of individual and state.

Marcus, rather, advises his readers to examine certain psychological mistakes and misconceptions that seem to regularly arise. For example: he invites his reader to treat the finality and universality of death as a means of liberation from anxiety rather than seeing it as the principal source of anxiety about existence that people are psychologically prone to.[6] He also urges his readers to view positive mental habits as tools that can subdue and direct unruly emotions. If, for instance, someone takes the correct attitude to an aspect of our experience, they should take note of that attitude and make every effort to cultivate it. At one point, he advises the reader to treat the philosophical wisdom contained in his treatise as a medical tool-kit.[7] The implication of the analogy is unmistakable: just as medical treatment can heal us physically, philosophical doctrines can provide people with a means of diagnosing and healing character and temperament and achieving a healthy balance of mind. Still, although it is clear that Marcus intends *Meditations* to be a guide and source of encouragement for practical living, few of his reflections can be described as formal statements of philosophical doctrines or principles.

In recent years, philosophers such as the French historian of ancient philosophy Pierre Hadot* have begun to revisit this approach. This is most evident in *Philosophy as a Way of Life* (1995), a book that describes at length the practical teachings of Epictetus* and Marcus Aurelius.[8]

Overlooked

One of the attractions of *Meditations* for many readers today is the way in which the text recommends a reflective and even spiritual way of life without appealing to external sources of authority, such as sacred texts or the institutions of the world's great religions. This has meant that the role played by piety in Marcus's thought has been relatively overlooked. His central notion is that the world is unfolding according to a providential plan or design, overseen by God, and will continue to do so regardless of the ways people might attempt to divert the stream of historical change. This is futile, he claims, and people should respond to whatever events occur in a spirit of acceptance, humility, and piety. Only then is it possible to attain the state of tranquil composure that is the true mark of the Stoic philosopher. Indeed, whether or not you are a follower of Stoic philosophy, Marcus believed that you should approach life by rising above the difficulties, misfortunes, and challenges you confront.

If the Stoics were correct to assert a strong doctrine of fatalism— that is, if the course of history is in some sense fixed—then clearly there is nothing that emotions of anger, grief, or fear can do to affect or change the outcome of a situation. Even if the doctrine is false, he notes,[9] the most plausible alternative—namely the one advanced by the Epicureans*—is that indivisible material particles move around completely randomly, in which case everything that happens is arbitrary and it remains futile to respond to the world in ways that imply any of us could change it.

NOTES

1   Marcus Aurelius, *Meditations: With Selected Correspondence*, trans. Robin Hard (Oxford: Oxford University Press, 2011), 10.11 and 12.1.

2   Plato, *Republic*, trans. Robin Waterfield (Oxford: Oxford University Press, 1993).

3   Marcus, *Meditations*, 8.7.

4   Marcus, *Meditations*, 7.55.

5   Marcus, *Meditations*, 5.16.

6   Marcus, *Meditations*, 4.50.

7   Marcus, *Meditations*, 3.13.

8   Pierre Hadot, *Philosophy as a Way of Life*, ed. Arnold I. Davidson, trans. Michael Chase (Oxford: Blackwell, 1995).

9   Marcus, *Meditations*, 8.17, 9.39.

MODULE 7
ACHIEVEMENT

KEY POINTS

- There is some tension in Marcus's thought between Stoicism* and its rival school, Epicureanism.*

- The advice given in *Meditations* appears to have benefited its author: Marcus ruled the Roman Empire* at a difficult time in its history, but appears to have done so relatively compassionately.

- The mystery surrounding the occasion and purpose of *Meditations* can make it a difficult text to interpret.

Assessing the Argument

As many of the reflections that make up Marcus Aurelius's *Meditations* are forms of practical and psychological advice, it is harder to pick out and evaluate a set of clear philosophical theses or doctrines from the text than is typically the case with other great contributions to the history of the philosophical tradition. Even so, there are ways of determining the strengths and weaknesses of the arguments that Marcus puts forward. Most obviously, unlike the overwhelming majority of philosophical works in the Western tradition, *Meditations* is a text that can be tested very simply by its readers; they need only follow its practical suggestions and apply them to their everyday lives to see if theirs is a peaceful and balanced state of mind.

One of the curious features of *Meditations*, however, is that it is sometimes difficult to identify whether its message should be assessed as a Stoic argument. At several points Marcus seems to leave open the question of whether or not Stoicism is the world view that his reader should endorse. For example, Marcus sets out

> ❝ A true and eternal gospel, the book of *Meditations* will never grow old, for it affirms no dogma ... [it] remains young with life and truth. ❞
>
> Ernest Renan, *Marcus Aurelius*

the two main accounts of fundamental reality on nine occasions in *Meditations*.[1] These can be summarized in Marcus's own belief in "providence or chance." Scholars have debated for years whether this suggests that Marcus was undecided on the question of whether the Stoic providence-based view of nature was to be preferred to the Epicurean chance-based view. It might be the case, as one scholar has suggested,[2] that Marcus wished to make the point that regardless of which theory of natural processes one prefers, it is the Stoic ethical life—and not the Epicurean one—that should be pursued.

Achievement in Context

Marcus stands as the last of a line of rulers of the Roman Empire who are sometimes referred to favorably as the "Five Good Emperors" of ancient Rome. These great leaders included Nerva* (96–98 c.e.), Trajan* (98–117 c.e), Hadrian* (117–38 c.e.), Antoninus Pius* (138–160 c.e.), and Marcus Aurelius (161–180 c.e.). But by composing *Meditations*, Marcus also achieved a place within the canon of Stoic philosophers. "Canon" here signifies the list of works considered the most important in the Stoic tradition; Marcus has a place in this canon even if the work lacks the learning and philosophical sharpness that defines others (in particular the writings of the philosophers Chrysippus* and Epictetus)* in the Greek intellectual tradition. What is remarkable about the achievement of *Meditations* is that it shows how the practical ethics of Stoicism could be applied in a life that would have imposed exceptional demands—administrative, political, and military.

The only other ancient texts that come close to achieving this level of success are Cicero's* *On Duties* (*De Officiis*), written around 44 B.C.E., and Seneca's* *On Anger* (*De Ira*), written in the late 30s C.E. Each of these provides advice on the qualities necessary for civic life, and each of them is composed by men who were major political figures. Like Cicero and Seneca, Marcus avoids giving specific autobiographical examples of how he applies the principles he recommends. The achievement of *Meditations* stands easy comparison with ancient and modern works—the highly influential Christian* religious philosopher Augustine's* *Confessions* or Pascal's* *Pensées*— that can also be seen as philosophical exercises carried out by means of introspective analysis and internal dialogue. It is the text that first marks what the French historian and philosopher Michel Foucault* described as a "turn to the self" in Western thought.[3]

Limitations

One of the principal difficulties posed by *Meditations* is knowing when and why it was written. It is not a work that appears to have been intended for a wider readership, and as a result has a degree of formlessness and can also appear to lack much sense of arguments logically organized. The absence of structure means that it can be difficult for the reader to grasp the complex interconnections between the themes on which Marcus focuses. The shapelessness of *Meditations* can also, therefore, make it a hard text to digest, even if this is partly compensated for by its concise, aphoristic style—it is composed of a series of relatively brief and compact paragraphs, each communicating an idea, in keeping with the brief texts known as "aphorisms."

Another of the weaknesses sometimes noted is the implausibility of the link Marcus suggests between a principle in Stoic natural philosophy and a principle in Stoic ethics: the idea that since every physical event is connected to every other physical event, every human being is connected to every other human being. In other words, Marcus underpins his theory of the universality of humanity with the thesis, drawn from Stoic physical science, that physical entities are also universally connected throughout the natural world.

NOTES

1   Marcus Aurelius, *Meditations: With Selected Correspondence*, trans. Robin Hard (Oxford: Oxford University Press, 2011), 4.3, 6.24, 7.32, 7.50, 8.17, 9.28, 11.39, 10.6, and 11.18.

2   Julia Annas, "Marcus Aurelius: Ethics and Its Background," *Rhizai* 2 (2004), 103–19.

3   Michel Foucault, *History of Sexuality, Vol. III: The Care of the Self* (New York: Pantheon, 1990), 39–52.

MODULE 8
PLACE IN THE AUTHOR'S WORK

KEY POINTS

- Since *Meditations* is the only work Marcus composed, the only source that it can be compared to is his correspondence with his tutor Marcus Cornelius Fronto.*

- Given that Marcus appears to have written *Meditations* with no reader in mind other than himself, it is curious that the work contains so little autobiographical information.

- Marcus comes closer than any other figure from the ancient world to embodying the philosopher Plato's* ideal of a philosopher-king.

Positioning

At one level, the task of positioning *Meditations* within Marcus Aurelius's body of work is straightforward: the only other work of his to have survived is his correspondence with his tutor Fronto, which was discovered only in 1815 on reused parchment in a library in Milan. Nevertheless, a comparison between *Meditations* and the surviving letters offers valuable insights not only into Marcus's personality but into his thinking. After all, *Meditations* itself—though very much an interior dialogue—reveals relatively little about how Marcus himself applied his principles of practical reasoning to his own daily life. Conversely, the letters reveal Marcus's affection for his tutor: he prays frequently that Fronto be relieved from the many health troubles from which he suffered and constantly stresses the extent of his personal and intellectual debts to him.[1]

Apart from *Meditations* and the correspondence with Fronto, there is no evidence from external sources that he wrote anything else.

66 Since there is no definite date concerning the chronology of the *Meditations*, it is impossible to assert that it is the work of a whole lifetime. Nevertheless, the fragmentary nature ... of the various chapters ... would lead us to think of a rather wide time span, maybe several years. 99

Matteo Ceporina, "The *Meditations*"

Given his position as emperor, however, it seems safe to assume that while *Meditations* may have been the only significant text that Marcus produced it is possible that he produced others that have not survived. Similarly, there is no way to determine how this text fits within the context of Marcus's career. What is known, though, is that most of *Meditations* was written during the time that Marcus was engaged in a military campaign in the region of Dalmatia, in modern-day Croatia.

Integration

Given its practical focus, one of the most puzzling features of *Meditations* is that Marcus makes no effort in it to relate the ethical principles he promotes to his own life. In this respect, it is very different from a work like *Confessions* by the influential fourth- and fifth-century Christian* scholar Augustine,* a work that otherwise resembles *Meditations* in a number of respects. In sharp contrast to Augustine, Marcus cultivates a curiously detached tone and almost never attempts to illustrate a philosophical or ethical point by citing an event from his own life that might serve as an example. This can be a source of frustration for his readers, since the work represents a rare insight into the mind of a major historical figure who, during the last decade or so of his life (that is, after the death of his co-regent Lucius Verus)* was the single most important and powerful ruler in the world.

Still, this need not imply that Marcus failed to integrate his philosophical world view into the demands of practical living but that, rather, he avoided making concrete applications of his philosophy to specific events in his daily life. There can be little doubt that this accounts for the enduring legacy of *Meditations*: the work retains a generality that means its ideas can be applied to the very different practical situations that have confronted (and continue to confront) its many readers.

Significance

There can be little doubt that *Meditations* is the most significant philosophical work by a major political figure of the ancient world. It is true that both Julius Caesar* and the politician and orator Cicero* composed many important works, but these focus primarily on rhetoric, history, and politics and do not achieve the depth or argumentative rigor that distinguishes *Meditations*.

In many ways the work embodies the ideal of a philosopher-ruler first proposed by Plato in his most famous dialogue, *Republic*. In it, Plato argued that those people who have immersed themselves in the discipline and practice of philosophy are in the best position to govern with wisdom and justice. It is not easy for modern scholars to determine the extent to which Marcus consciously pursued this ambition. Nor is it clear whether he did, in fact, ensure that Stoic philosophical principles informed the military and administrative decisions he took as emperor of Rome. Few would deny though that over the course of the long history of philosophy and politics in the ancient world, no one came closer to meeting Plato's ideal of the philosopher-king than Marcus himself. He was neither the greatest emperor to rule the Roman Empire* nor the greatest or most original interpreter of Stoic philosophy, but his mastery of both politics and philosophy ranks as an achievement that has no equal or parallel in the Greco-Roman world.

NOTES

1   Marcus Cornelius Fronto, *Correspondence of Marcus Cornelius Fronto with Marcus Aurelius Antoninus, Lucius Verus, Antoninus Pius, and Various Friends*, trans. C. R. Haines (Cambridge, MA: Harvard University Press, 1919), 3.10–11.

SECTION 3
IMPACT

MODULE 9
THE FIRST RESPONSES

KEY POINTS

- Due to its history, reactions to *Meditations* were rare and intermittent for over 1000 years after its composition.

- After its rediscovery and publication in the sixteenth century, however, the work began to exercise a wide-ranging influence.

- Few points of contention have arisen in the scholarly interpretation of *Meditations*.

Criticism

In the centuries after its composition, Marcus Aurelius's *Meditations* appears to have disappeared almost entirely from view. There are two or three glancing references to *Meditations* in the fourth and ninth centuries, but these do not amount to anything that could be described as critical engagement. The most plausible explanation for the critical silence is, of course, that the work was never intended to be read by anyone other than Marcus himself. It is clear that the text was not circulated within Marcus's lifetime, and copies only began to appear many centuries later. There is very little evidence, in fact, that it was even known as *Meditations*. For example, in the fourth century the text was referred to as the "Instructions" of Marcus Aurelius.

Another reason for the critical silence that greeted *Meditations* is that most early medieval* thinkers could not read Greek. So within the context of ancient and medieval thought, it is safe to conclude that there is no history of the reception of *Meditations* to be written. Nevertheless, the work reappeared in Europe at some point in the

❝[Marcus Aurelius's] writings [are] the highest
ethical product of the ancient mind.**❞**
John Stuart Mill, *On Liberty and Other Writings*

fifteenth century, probably as a result of the migration of scholars to
continental Europe after the conquest of Constantinople (present-
day Istanbul) by the Ottoman Empire* in 1453. It was a Swiss
scholar who first prepared an edition of *Meditations* in 1558 (he
named the work *To Himself*), and it was translated into Latin over the
following decade. After this, the work slipped into the bloodstream
of European philosophical and political thought, though mostly as a
source of practical advice. It has only rarely been considered a text
for which critical engagement is appropriate.

Responses

Once printed translations of *Meditations* began to circulate more
widely, many of its guiding themes and ideas begin to emerge
in a remarkably broad number of other works. However, it is its
influence on a particular tradition in moral philosophy known as
the sentimentalist tradition that is most evident. The British moral
philosopher Anthony Ashley Cooper, 3rd Earl of Shaftesbury,*
writing in the late seventeenth and early eighteenth centuries,
described *Meditations* as "the testimony of one of the wisest and
most serious of ancient authors, whose single authority would be
acknowledged to have equal force with that of many concurring
writers."[1]

Shaftesbury's most influential successor was the moral
philosopher Francis Hutcheson* (1694–1746), a man who shared
his predecessor's ambition to develop an idea of moral philosophy
in which emotion and sentiment were more central than cognitive
reason. In particular, Hutcheson identified in *Meditations* a welcome

emphasis on the universal scope of the requirements of justice as applicable to every human being by virtue of his or her membership of the species. Hutcheson adopts the basic stance that Marcus takes toward the question of the intrinsic moral character of human beings, arguing against the emphasis of Western Christian* religious thought on the doctrine of original sin (the principle that human beings are inherently and definitively tainted, morally speaking, by the sinful actions of Eve in the Garden of Eden, as set out in the first biblical book *Genesis*). In contrast to this position, Hutcheson attempts again and again to argue that human beings are by nature benevolent and good. It is clear that Marcus also exerted a considerable influence on Hutcheson's account of the nature of good will, truth, and the role of the intellect.

Conflict and Consensus

There are almost no writers who have seen *Meditations* negatively or critically. In general, the few conflicts the work has stimulated tend to arise as a result of the difficulties involved in characterizing the genre, style, and content of the work. One of the central issues of critical inquiry into *Meditations* is the extent to which it is consistent with mainstream Stoic* philosophy. The French historian Pierre Hadot* has argued that Marcus draws a distinction between judgments about objective, physical facts on the one hand and judgments about value on the other in a way that departs from the orthodox Stoic claim that judgments about beauty, goodness, and virtue are value judgments about the way the world is; they are not founded on our various capacities to recognize the way the world operates.[2]

Another point of contention turns on the question of whether the mind bears the stamp and character of sense-impressions: the things it perceives. At one point, it is clear that Marcus believes this to be the case.[3] However, it is plausible to suppose that such sense-experience is fundamentally involuntary. If the mind owes its development and formation to sense-impressions, and if these arise involuntarily, then our mental activity must also be involuntary, which would render meaningless the repeated commands in *Meditations* to use the mind as the "governing center" of the self.[4]

NOTES

1   Earl of Shaftesbury (Anthony Ashley Cooper), *Characteristics of Men, Manners, Opinions, Times*, ed. Laurence E. Klein (Cambridge: Cambridge University Press, 1999), 113.

2   Pierre Hadot, *The Inner Citadel: The* Meditations *of Marcus Aurelius*, trans. Michael Chase (Cambridge, MA: Harvard University Press, 1998), 103–4.

3   Marcus Aurelius, *Meditations: With Selected Correspondence*, trans. Robin Hard (Oxford: Oxford University Press, 2011), 5.16.

4   Marcus, *Meditations*, 2.2, 5.26, 5.33, 12.3.

MODULE 10
THE EVOLVING DEBATE

KEY POINTS

- Scholarly debate about *Meditations* continues to center on the question of its genre and structure.

- Elements of the approach that Marcus Aurelius adopts in *Meditations* can be detected in a number of other influential texts in the centuries after its rediscovery.

- Contemporary enthusiasm for *Meditations* can be attributed to a revival of interest in the approach of some ancient thinkers to treating philosophy as a guide to living.

Uses and Problems

Given its almost complete absence from the history of Western thought for more than 1,400 years between its composition in the second century C.E. and its eventual circulation in the sixteenth century, the ideas that are most distinctive of Marcus Aurelius's *Meditations* have been used, reproduced, and criticized fairly infrequently. Many of its ideas persist, of course, in the writings of those who shared with Marcus the basic Stoic* outlook on reality. But one problematic and recurring feature of many interpretations of *Meditations* since its retrieval and publication in the sixteenth century is puzzlement over the organization and structure of the work. Indeed when it was published in 1558 (with an accompanying translation into Latin), its editor speculated that *Meditations* was in fact a disconnected series of extracts from a much larger work that Marcus had composed.

A similar conclusion was drawn in the seventeenth century. More recently, however, interpreters have come to accept that

❝ It is in Marcus Aurelius that one finds the clearest formulation of an experience of political power that, on the one hand, takes the form of an occupation separate from status and, on the other, requires the careful practice of personal virtues. ❞

Michel Foucault,* *History of Sexuality, Vol. III: The Care of the Self*

Meditations was composed largely in its current form, and that it is best understood as a collection of personal notes (known in Greek as *hypomnemata* or "recollections"), although the work does otherwise differ from similar collections of its kind in important ways.[1] In particular, it appears that *Meditations* was intended to be used as a set of spiritual exercises for the sole improvement of its author.

Schools of Thought

Although *Meditations* has not given rise to any distinctive schools of thought, it remains one of the best and most accessible accounts of Stoic philosophy. Both its methodology and its approach find parallels among works such as Blaise Pascal's* *Pensées* and *Spiritual Exercises* by the sixteenth-century religious scholar Ignatius of Loyola,* though there is no evidence that either Pascal or Ignatius were consciously imitating *Meditations* (impossible in any case in the case of Ignatius, since his *Spiritual Exercises* were composed several decades before *Meditations* was published). The resemblance to representative thinkers of the Christian* tradition is not accidental, since it is clear that *Meditations* is best understood as a text that aims to guide the spiritual formation of its reader. As a result, it invites its reader to recognize the proper relationship between God on the one hand and material (physical) and immaterial reality on the other ("immaterial reality" is that which cannot be perceived, but is nevertheless real: thought, angels, number, souls, sets, and so on).

Within Stoic theology,* God is understood very differently from the theology of the Abrahamic faiths (Judaism,* Christianity, and Islam*). In particular, Abrahamic theism conceives God in personal terms ("He," "Him") and insists upon a clear distinction between God as creator and the world as created. That said, Stoicism is a philosophy committed to the existence of a divine reality—it is, in other words, committed to the claim that God exists and is continually engaged in the world. What it rejects is the claim of the Abrahamic faiths that God is *distinct* from the natural world; instead, Stoics understand God to be the force (the rational principle, perhaps) that animates physical reality and exercises control over it that we understand as providence, or fate.

In Current Scholarship

Much of the recent scholarly work on *Meditations* focuses on the way in which it advocates a practical philosophy and avoids an abstract theoretical system. Similarly, in modern times we only need to glance at the titles of books on best seller lists to recognize that there is an enormous popular appetite for understanding the practical benefits that the study of philosophy can bring. Perhaps the most influential figure in current scholarship on *Meditations* and its distinctively pragmatic approach to philosophical inquiry is the French philosopher and historian of late antiquity Pierre Hadot.* Hadot was heavily influenced early on in his career by the British Austrian philosopher Ludwig Wittgenstein's* *Philosophical Investigations* (1953), a text that many cite as a champion of an anti-theoretical approach to philosophy, and—in particular—the idea that apparently profound philosophical problems should be resolved not by theoretical inquiry but by practicing philosophy as if it were a form of therapeutic exercise. This is the central assertion of Hadot's extremely influential book *Philosophy as a Way of Life* (1995). It is no less a dominant, recurring theme in his *The Inner Citadel: The*

Meditations of Marcus Aurelius (1992), an important study devoted exclusively to *Meditations*.

NOTES

1   Matteo Ceporina, "The *Meditations,*" in *A Companion to Marcus Aurelius*, ed. Marcel van Ackeren (Chichester: Wiley-Blackwell, 2012).

MODULE 11
IMPACT AND INFLUENCE TODAY

KEY POINTS

- *Meditations* has enjoyed a remarkable renaissance of interest in recent decades.

- The renewal of enthusiasm has partly arisen because it challenges the idea that philosophy is an exclusively theoretical discipline, proposing instead that it is a tool to help one live one's life.

- The challenge has been taken up by a number of thinkers who champion a shift to what has been labeled an "anti-philosophical" conception of philosophy.

Position

Today, for specialists and nonspecialists alike, Marcus Aurelius's *Meditations* tends to be held up as putting forward a new idea of philosophy as a way of life. The work of the French historian Pierre Hadot* in particular has been welcomed as a bracing, acute, and historically informed assault on the theoretical pretentions of much contemporary academic philosophy. There is a growing scholarly trend in support of the view that *Meditations* should be seen within a long tradition of thought in the antique world, the world of Greece and Rome, in which philosophical inquiry should structure and guide practical living. The central idea, in other words, is that the practice of ancient philosophy more closely resembled what we would understand as a religious way of life than the practice of contemporary academic philosophy.

Nevertheless, the idea that philosophy should be conducted *exclusively* as a practical discipline to prepare people for the demands

❝I did read [*Meditations*] on many occasions. And
I was very deeply impressed by the words that he
wrote in the book to the effect that, where are those
people who were great for a time? They are all gone,
living only a story, or some even just half a story. So,
I draw the conclusion that only people are in the
position to create history and to write history.**❞**

Wen Jiabao,* Interview with *Newsweek*

of daily life is unlikely to have been one that Marcus would have
endorsed, even though it is clear that *Meditations* is cited by scholarly
and popular writers alike to lend the authority of antiquity to the
view that philosophy should be a practical exercise. Indeed, it is a
remarkable feature of the contemporary reception of *Meditations*
that almost no historian or scholar has offered any serious objections
to the principles and world view that it urges its readers to adopt.

Interaction

It is now widely recognized that *Meditations* demonstrates the
continuing strength and resilience of Stoicism's* ethical ideas.
Indeed, these days no ancient text is considered a more succinct or
comprehensive account of Stoicism than *Meditations*, even if it is also
true that Seneca's* ethical treatises and Epictetus's* *Discourses* and
Enchiridion continue to be held in very high regard. This represents
a dramatic departure from the seventeenth and eighteenth centuries,
a period when very few scholars treated *Meditations* as representative
of the Stoic philosophical tradition. It's ironic that the work is
more popular today that the texts most commentators would
have deemed the greatest in the Stoic canon; many scholars would
consider *Meditations* to lack the degree or depth of philosophical
insight and sophistication that characterizes the works of the great

Stoic philosophers, from which it derives. Nevertheless, it is very likely that the legacy of the work will continue to grow in the future, not least because it provides a model of someone who was able to combine a position of global leadership with philosophically serious and plausible reflections on the place and role of humans in the natural world.

The Continuing Debate

A striking number of contemporary political figures have engaged with and derived much value from the advice that Marcus offers in *Meditations*. It has been claimed that the former president of the United States Bill Clinton,* for example, rereads the book every year or two.[1] Similarly, it emerged a few years ago that Wen Jiabao,* a former premier of the People's Republic of China, has read *Meditations* a hundred times, claiming in an interview with *Newsweek* that he "was very deeply impressed by the words that he wrote in the book; I very much value morality, and I do believe that entrepreneurs, economists and statesmen alike should pay much more attention to morality and ethics."[2] Wen's remarks are consistent with the recurring emphasis in many of his speeches that finance and enterprise must be conducted in ways that are consistent with the demands of individual morality and social justice. It is also true that *Meditations* provides its modern readers with a way of understanding how human freedom is possible within a framework that ultimately presupposes determinism*—according to which there is nothing we can do to alter the unfolding of history. This point is especially important given the assertion by some that human freedom is no longer a plausible notion in view of the fact that there is evidence that human behavior is nothing but the visible face of evolutionary, economic, and psychological forces.

NOTES

1   William H. Honan, "Books, Books and More Books: Clinton an Omnivorous Reader," *The New York Times*, December 10, 1992, accessed November 26, 2015, http://www.nytimes.com/1992/12/10/books/books-books-and-more-books-clinton-an-omnivorous-reader.html?pagewanted=all.

2   Fareed Zakaria, "Chinese Prime Minister Wen Jiabao Interviewed," *Newsweek*, September 30, 2008, accessed November 26, 2015, http://www.newsweek.com/chinese-prime-minister-wen-jiabao-interviewed-89187.

MODULE 12
WHERE NEXT?

KEY POINTS

- In many ways, the enduring popularity of *Meditations* can be attributed to the Western appetite for self-improvement literature.

- In the future, *Meditations* is likely to be increasingly exploited as a resource for education in business and leadership.

- It is a safe assumption that *Meditations* will continue to excite fascination in popular and academic culture.

Potential

The importance of Marcus Aurelius's *Meditations* was evident in 1995 when one of the world's great publishers, Penguin Books, celebrated its 60th anniversary. To commemorate this milestone, it released 60 short books; *Meditations* was among them. The work turned out to be one of Penguin's best selling books of the year. More than two decades on, the text continues to influence a wide range of highly influential figures across the world. It is likely to continue to exert a similar influence in the decades ahead. There has also been a striking growth of interest in ideas surrounding the notion of *leadership* in political, business, and management circles. In particular, a great degree of energy will continue to be expended on the problem of how to emphasize ethical leadership in a global society, and in particular on the kind of exercises and training that might contribute to the formation of virtuous character. If we take seriously the deep and diverse impact that the work has had both on political leaders and ordinary readers in the past few decades, it is difficult to imagine that

> **❝** As Marcus receives more attention from specialists and the details of his position become clearer, the old caricatures that have shaped much of the recent reception will no longer be tenable. **❞**
>
> John Sellars, "Marcus Aurelius in Contemporary Philosophy"

the ideas related in *Meditations* will fail to play some role in the many debates and discussions related to this problem in the future.

Future Directions

Although Pierre Hadot,* one of the greatest exponents of philosophy as a practical exercise, died in 2010, his work has inspired a new generation of historians of ideas and political philosophers to excavate *Meditations* for fresh ways of thinking about the relationship between ethics, politics, and philosophy. It is likely that *Meditations* will continue to be one of the most important resources for anyone reflecting on the challenges of ethical leadership. In particular, Marcus's repeated emphasis on the importance of adopting a reflective and balanced sense of self-awareness has obvious parallels with the contemporary enthusiasm for the practice of mindfulness,* a concept that has attracted a great deal of popular and academic interest in recent years. It is essentially a meditative practice of the Buddhist* religious tradition that has been popularized very successfully in the West. There are, of course, many important differences between Buddhist and Stoic* ethical teachings. But in terms of practical advice, the notion of ethics as a primarily *therapeutic* discipline is one both have in common. Since *Meditations* takes very seriously the importance of developing a balanced and reflective mindset through practicing a careful analysis of one's emotions and desires, it is likely to become an important and influential resource for the mindfulness movement.

Summary

In sum, a strong case can be made that *Meditations* stands out as one of the most important and influential philosophical works from antiquity. Nearly two thousand years after Marcus decided to start his notebook of personal reflections, *Meditations* continues to be read by contemporary moral and political philosophers, by figures in positions of global influence, and by those with little knowledge of the ancient world or of Stoicism as a philosophical system. It will do so for many of the same reasons that it was read and reread after its rediscovery in the sixteenth century. The most important of these must include its intensely practical focus, its repeated emphasis on the importance of self-awareness, and its unrelenting attention to the importance of putting day-to-day misfortunes in their proper context. It is true that few contemporary readers will be attracted to the deep commitment to the providential (fateful) and deterministic* unfolding of the world that is so central to the philosophy of Stoicism and to *Meditations* itself; even so, there are several thinkers who have claimed that history does indeed have a rational and discernible direction. There can be little doubt that the themes of *Meditations* will continue to provoke much interest in today's world, and could prove a notably valuable tool for anyone in search of a balanced, rational, and fruitful life.

GLOSSARIES

GLOSSARY OF TERMS

Aristotelianism: a tradition of Western philosophy inspired by the thought of the fourth century B.C.E. Greek philosopher Aristotle, a thinker best known for founding a number of fields of intellectual inquiry, including biology, psychology, political and literary theory, and logic.

Ataraxia: a Greek term employed in the philosophy of Epicureanism to denote a state of unruffled tranquility (or, more literally translated, "freedom from confusion").

Buddhism: a term encompassing a variety of religious and philosophical traditions rooted in the life and teachings of Siddh rtha Gautama (Buddha).

Christianity: a religion based on the life and teachings of Jesus of Nazareth in the first century C.E.; it is the largest religion in the world.

Cosmopolitanism: one of Stoicism's most influential ideas, cosmopolitanism stressed the universality and interconnectedness of human beings.

Determinism: in the context of historical processes and events, the view that free human agency has no part to play in historical change: everything unfolds by necessity.

Dualism: in the context of the philosophy of mind, an independent subdiscipline within contemporary philosophy dealing with matters related to the nature of consciousness and thought, dualism is the view that the mind and body are two irreducibly distinct categories of entity.

Epicureanism: an ancient tradition of philosophical thought inspired by the teachings of the philosopher Epicurus of Athens (341–270 B.C.E.).

Equestrian order: a social class of "knights" (*equites*) in ancient Rome that represented the lower of the two aristocratic classes.

Eudaimonism: an ethical theory inspired by the teachings of Aristotle that took human flourishing to be the central goal of human life and ethical reasoning.

Fatalism: a view commonly associated with Stoic philosophy, according to which historical change and human agency are controlled by fate.

Islam: a religion whose followers worship Allah as the only God, and that bases itself on the word of the Qur'an and the teachings of the prophet Mohammed.

Judaism: a religion believing in one God that originated in the Middle East and traces its beginnings back three thousand years. Christianity emerged from one of the many different Jewish movements that existed in the first century C.E.

Materialism: the view that matter is the only constitutive ingredient of reality.

Medieval period: also known as the Middle Ages, this is generally considered to last from the fifth to the fifteenth century. It is so called as it is the middle of the three common divisions in European history: the Classical period, the Middle Ages, and the modern period.

Mindfulness: a meditative practice and contemplative attitude inspired by Buddhist teachings.

Ottoman Empire: an empire founded in 1299; centered on present-day Turkey, at its height it ruled significant territories in North Africa, Western Asia, and Southern Europe. It was dissolved in 1922.

Patrician class: a leading aristocratic class in Rome during the Republican and Imperial periods.

Platonism: the tradition of Western philosophy inspired by the thought of the Greek philosopher Plato and best known for developing an account of the physical world as reflecting a transcendent system of reality that lies beyond space and time.

Renaissance: a term first coined in the nineteenth century to describe a period in Western literature, arts, and culture from the fourteenth to the seventeenth century that witnessed a resurgence of interest in the Greco-Roman heritage of Europe.

Roman Empire: the principal political, economic, and military structure of the Roman civilization that lasted from the fall of the Republic and the rise of its first emperor Caesar Augustus in the last quarter of the first century B.C.E. and continued until its slow decline during the fifth century C.E.

Salii: a priestly class in ancient Rome made of 12 aristocratic young men who participated in ceremonies dressed in the clothing and military paraphernalia of archaic warriors.

Scottish Enlightenment: a period in eighteenth-century Scotland that emphasized a rationalist and humanist approach to philosophical and political problems, and whose most famous figures included David Hume, Adam Ferguson, Thomas Reid, Adam Smith, and Francis Hutcheson.

Stoicism: a highly influential tradition of Greco-Roman philosophy first associated with philosophers who taught in the Stoa at Athens and whose most famous exponents include Zeno, Chrysippus, Epictetus, Seneca the Younger, and Marcus Aurelius. It was a system of thought that prized rationality as the animating principle of reality and that emphasized the importance of mastering the nonrational aspects of the human person

Theology: the study of religious principles, commonly conducted through commentary on religious texts.

Umayyad Caliphate: a system of theocratic government instituted early on in the history of Islam in 661 C.E., just under 30 years after the death of Mohammed in 632 C.E.

PEOPLE MENTIONED IN THE TEXT

Apollonius of Tyre was a Greek Stoic philosopher who contributed to the transmission of Stoic philosophy to the Roman world.

Aristotle (384–322 B.C.E.) was a pupil of Plato and tutor to Alexander the Great. He founded a philosophical school known as the Lyceum and wrote works that qualify him as perhaps the greatest philosopher of antiquity.

Arrian (c. 86–c.140/160 C.E.) was a Roman philosopher and historian from the region of Bithynia in modern-day Turkey.

Augustine of Hippo (354–430 C.E.) was a theologian and bishop, and one of the two or three most influential theologians in Western Christian theology.

Chrysippus (279–206 B.C.E.) was a Greek philosopher widely acknowledged to be the second founder of Stoicism after Zeno of Citium.

Marcus Tullius Cicero (106–43 B.C.E.) was a Roman politician, philosopher, lawyer, and orator, and one of the greatest ever writers of Latin prose.

Bill Clinton (b. 1946) was a Democratic president of the United States between 1993 and 2001.

Commodus (161–192 C.E.) was the son of Marcus Aurelius and became a tyrannical emperor of Rome between his father's death in 180 C.E. and his own in 192 C.E.

Anthony Ashley Cooper, 3rd Earl of Shaftesbury (1671–1713) was a writer, diplomat, moral philosopher, politician, and traveler.

Democritus (460–370 B.C.E.) was a Greek philosopher from Abdera in Thrace who was the first thinker to develop an atomistic theory of reality.

René Descartes (1596–1650) was a French philosopher, physicist, and mathematician, widely considered the father of modern philosophy.

Epictetus (55–135 C.E.) was a Greek-born philosopher of Stoicism and author of *Discourses* and *Enchiridion*, two influential and widely admired expositions of Stoic philosophy.

Epicurus (341–270 B.C.E.) was a major philosopher of the ancient world who lived, studied, and taught in Athens, where he also founded a school that bore his name. He is best known for his view that reality was wholly material, that human life should be ordered toward what is most pleasurable for the individual, and that even though the gods do exist they do not providentially intervene with the course of the world.

Rupilia Faustina (87–138 C.E.) was a Roman aristocrat who, as grandmother of Marcus Aurelius, established his link to the imperial household.

Michel Foucault (1926–84) was an influential French philosopher, social historian, and historian of ideas, who authored several important genealogical investigations.

Marcus Cornelius Fronto (c. 100–170 C.E.) was a Roman senator and consul who, as a tutor to the young Marcus Aurelius, exercised an important intellectual influence on him.

Pierre Hadot (1922–2010) was a French historian and scholar of ancient philosophy, and exponent of the influential thesis that ancient philosophy was primarily intended to provide advice on how to live one's life.

Hadrian (76–138 C.E.) was a Roman emperor regarded as one of the so-called "Five Emperors" who was responsible for rebuilding the Pantheon in Rome.

Heraclitus (c. 535–c. 475 B.C.E.) was a so-called pre-Socratic Greek philosopher from Ephesus in modern-day Turkey who is perhaps best known for his stress on the importance of constant change in his natural philosophy.

Homer (c. 800–c. 701 B.C.E.) was the author of the *Iliad* and the *Odyssey*, and perhaps the most important early figure in the history of Western literature.

David Hume (1711–76) was a Scottish philosopher and historian, one of the leading figures of the Scottish Enlightenment.

Francis Hutcheson (1694–1746) was a Scottish Irish philosopher interested in the role of feeling and sentiment in moral inquiry and was, with David Hume, one of the leading figures in the Scottish Enlightenment.

Ignatius of Loyola (1491–1556), originally known as Inigo Lopez, was a Spanish knight and soldier who underwent a religious experience, studied theology in Spain and at the Sorbonne in Paris before founding the Society of Jesus in 1539 (more generally known as the Jesuits), a major movement in the Roman Catholic Church's response to the Reformation.

Wen Jiabao (b. 1942) was premier of the People's Republic of China from 2003 to 2013.

Niccolò Machiavelli (1469–1527) was an Italian philosopher and diplomat, best known as the author of *The Prince*. He argued that the use of force and immoral behavior are sometimes necessary to retain power, and that no means should be spared to achieve this end.

Nerva (30–98 C.E.) was a Roman emperor and founder of the Nerva–Antonine dynasty who, despite his brief reign from 96 to 98 C.E., gained a reputation for wisdom and moderation.

Blaise Pascal (1623–62) was one of the most influential French philosophers of the seventeenth century and one of the greatest mathematicians of all time.

Antoninus Pius (86–161 C.E.) was the immediate predecessor to Marcus Aurelius. He ruled successfully as emperor between 138 and 161 C.E., and was an important influence on his successor.

Plato (c. 429–c. 347 B.C.E.) was an Athenian philosopher, metaphysician, and mathematician. He was a pupil of Socrates, teacher of Aristotle, and founder of the Academy—a famously influential school of philosophy.

Richard Rorty (1931–2007) was an influential philosopher based in the US university of Princeton who worked initially in the Anglo-American tradition, but whose *Philosophy and the Mirror of Nature* (1979) came to represent an important critique of that tradition and marked the renewal of American pragmatism.

Musonius Rufus (c. 20–c. 101 c.e.) was a Roman philosopher and teacher of Epictetus who was an important figure in the Stoic intellectual tradition shortly before Marcus Aurelius.

Quintus Junius Rusticus (100–170 c.e.) was one of Marcus Aurelius's teachers and the most respected Stoic philosopher in the lifetime of his most famous pupil.

Seneca the Younger (4 b.c.e.–65 c.e.) was a Roman Stoic philosopher, politician, playwright, and teacher and subsequently adviser to the emperor Nero, who eventually forced him to commit suicide for his alleged complicity in an assassination plot.

Adam Smith (1723–90) was the author of *The Theory of Moral Sentiments* (1759) and *An Inquiry into the Causes of the Wealth of Nations* (1776). As a moral philosopher, Smith is considered by many to be the father of the branch of economics known as "political economy."

Socrates (c. 470–399 b.c.e.) was an ancient Athenian who through the writings of his student Plato is now widely recognized as one of the foundational figures of Western philosophy.

Trajan (53–117 c.e.) was a Spanish-born Roman emperor, military commander, and civilian administrator.

Lucius Verus (130–169 C.E.) was a Roman politician, military commander, and co-emperor with Marcus Aurelius.

Ludwig Wittgenstein (1889–1951) was an Austrian-born philosopher of logic, language, and aesthetics, and author of *Tractatus Logico-Philosophicus* (1921) and *Philosophical Investigations* (1953), two highly influential works in twentieth-century philosophy.

Zeno of Citium (c. 334–c. 262 B.C.E.) was a Cypriot philosopher and founder of the Stoic school of philosophy in Athens in approximately 300 B.C.E.

WORKS CITED

WORKS CITED

Annas, Julia. "Marcus Aurelius: Ethics and its Background." *Rhizai* 2 (2004): 103–19.

Ceporina, Matteo. "The *Meditations*." In *A Companion to Marcus Aurelius*, edited by Marcel van Ackeren. Chichester: Wiley-Blackwell, 2012.

Epictetus, *The Discourses of Epictetus*. Translated by Robin Hard. London: Everyman, 1995.

Foucault, Michel. *History of Sexuality, Vol. III: The Care of the Self*. Translated by Robert Hurley. New York: Pantheon, 1990.

Fronto, Marcus Cornelius. *Correspondence of Marcus Cornelius Fronto with Marcus Aurelius Antoninus, Lucius Verus, Antoninus Pius, and Various Friends*. Translated by C. R. Haines. Cambridge, MA: Harvard University Press, 1919.

Hadot, Pierre. *The Inner Citadel: The* Meditations *of Marcus Aurelius*. Translated by Michael Chase. Cambridge, MA: Harvard University Press, 1998.

— — —. *Philosophy as a Way of Life*. Edited by Arnold I. Davidson. Translated by Michael Chase. Oxford: Blackwell, 1995.

Honan, William H. "Books, Books and More Books: Clinton an Omnivorous Reader." *The New York Times*, December 10, 1992. Accessed November 26, 2015. http://www.nytimes.com/1992/12/10/books/books-books-and-more-books-clinton-an-omnivorous-reader.html?pagewanted=all.

Marcus Aurelius. *Meditations: With Selected Correspondence*. Translated by Robin Hard. Oxford: Oxford University Press, 2011.

McLynn, Frank. *Marcus Aurelius: Warrior, Philosopher, Emperor*. London: Random House, 2009.

Mill, John Stuart. *On Liberty and Other Writings*. Edited by Stefan Collini. Cambridge: Cambridge University Press, 1989.

Plato, *Republic*. Translated by Robin Waterfield. Oxford: Oxford University Press, 1993.

Renan, Ernest. *Marcus Aurelius*. Translated by W. G. Hutchison. London: Walter Scott, 1904.

Rorty, Richard. *Philosophy and the Mirror of Nature*. Princeton, NJ: Princeton University Press, 1979.

Sellars, John. "Marcus Aurelius in Contemporary Philosophy." In *A Companion to Marcus Aurelius*, edited by Marcel van Ackeren, 532–44. Chichester: Wiley-Blackwell, 2012.

Shaftesbury, Earl of (Anthony Ashley Cooper). *Characteristics of Men, Manners, Opinions, Times*. Edited by Laurence E. Klein. Cambridge: Cambridge University Press, 1999.

Zakaria, Fareed. "Chinese Prime Minister Wen Jiabao Interviewed." *Newsweek*, September 30, 2008. Accessed November 26, 2015. http://www.newsweek.com/chinese-prime-minister-wen-jiabao-interviewed-89187.

THE MACAT LIBRARY
BY DISCIPLINE

AFRICANA STUDIES

Chinua Achebe's *An Image of Africa: Racism in Conrad's Heart of Darkness*
W. E. B. Du Bois's *The Souls of Black Folk*
Zora Neale Huston's *Characteristics of Negro Expression*
Martin Luther King Jr's *Why We Can't Wait*
Toni Morrison's *Playing in the Dark: Whiteness in the American Literary Imagination*

ANTHROPOLOGY

Arjun Appadurai's *Modernity at Large: Cultural Dimensions of Globalisation*
Philippe Ariès's *Centuries of Childhood*
Franz Boas's *Race, Language and Culture*
Kim Chan & Renée Mauborgne's *Blue Ocean Strategy*
Jared Diamond's *Guns, Germs & Steel: the Fate of Human Societies*
Jared Diamond's *Collapse: How Societies Choose to Fail or Survive*
E. E. Evans-Pritchard's *Witchcraft, Oracles and Magic Among the Azande*
James Ferguson's *The Anti-Politics Machine*
Clifford Geertz's *The Interpretation of Cultures*
David Graeber's *Debt: the First 5000 Years*
Karen Ho's *Liquidated: An Ethnography of Wall Street*
Geert Hofstede's *Culture's Consequences: Comparing Values, Behaviors, Institutes and Organizations across Nations*
Claude Lévi-Strauss's *Structural Anthropology*
Jay Macleod's *Ain't No Makin' It: Aspirations and Attainment in a Low-Income Neighborhood*
Saba Mahmood's *The Politics of Piety: The Islamic Revival and the Feminist Subjec*t
Marcel Mauss's *The Gift*

BUSINESS

Jean Lave & Etienne Wenger's *Situated Learning*
Theodore Levitt's *Marketing Myopia*
Burton G. Malkiel's *A Random Walk Down Wall Street*
Douglas McGregor's *The Human Side of Enterprise*
Michael Porter's *Competitive Strategy: Creating and Sustaining Superior Performance*
John Kotter's *Leading Change*
C. K. Prahalad & Gary Hamel's *The Core Competence of the Corporation*

CRIMINOLOGY

Michelle Alexander's *The New Jim Crow: Mass Incarceration in the Age of Colorblindness*
Michael R. Gottfredson & Travis Hirschi's *A General Theory of Crime*
Richard Herrnstein & Charles A. Murray's *The Bell Curve: Intelligence and Class Structure in American Life*
Elizabeth Loftus's *Eyewitness Testimony*
Jay Macleod's *Ain't No Makin' It: Aspirations and Attainment in a Low-Income Neighborhood*
Philip Zimbardo's *The Lucifer Effect*

ECONOMICS

Janet Abu-Lughod's *Before European Hegemony*
Ha-Joon Chang's *Kicking Away the Ladder*
David Brion Davis's *The Problem of Slavery in the Age of Revolution*
Milton Friedman's *The Role of Monetary Policy*
Milton Friedman's *Capitalism and Freedom*
David Graeber's *Debt: the First 5000 Years*
Friedrich Hayek's *The Road to Serfdom*
Karen Ho's *Liquidated: An Ethnography of Wall Street*

John Maynard Keynes's *The General Theory of Employment, Interest and Money*
Charles P. Kindleberger's *Manias, Panics and Crashes*
Robert Lucas's *Why Doesn't Capital Flow from Rich to Poor Countries?*
Burton G. Malkiel's *A Random Walk Down Wall Street*
Thomas Robert Malthus's *An Essay on the Principle of Population*
Karl Marx's *Capital*
Thomas Piketty's *Capital in the Twenty-First Century*
Amartya Sen's *Development as Freedom*
Adam Smith's *The Wealth of Nations*
Nassim Nicholas Taleb's *The Black Swan: The Impact of the Highly Improbable*
Amos Tversky's & Daniel Kahneman's *Judgment under Uncertainty: Heuristics and Biases*
Mahbub Ul Haq's *Reflections on Human Development*
Max Weber's *The Protestant Ethic and the Spirit of Capitalism*

FEMINISM AND GENDER STUDIES

Judith Butler's *Gender Trouble*
Simone De Beauvoir's *The Second Sex*
Michel Foucault's *History of Sexuality*
Betty Friedan's *The Feminine Mystique*
Saba Mahmood's *The Politics of Piety: The Islamic Revival and the Feminist Subject*
Joan Wallach Scott's *Gender and the Politics of History*
Mary Wollstonecraft's *A Vindication of the Rights of Woman*
Virginia Woolf's *A Room of One's Own*

GEOGRAPHY

The Brundtland Report's *Our Common Future*
Rachel Carson's *Silent Spring*
Charles Darwin's *On the Origin of Species*
James Ferguson's *The Anti-Politics Machine*
Jane Jacobs's *The Death and Life of Great American Cities*
James Lovelock's *Gaia: A New Look at Life on Earth*
Amartya Sen's *Development as Freedom*
Mathis Wackernagel & William Rees's *Our Ecological Footprint*

HISTORY

Janet Abu-Lughod's *Before European Hegemony*
Benedict Anderson's *Imagined Communities*
Bernard Bailyn's *The Ideological Origins of the American Revolution*
Hanna Batatu's *The Old Social Classes And The Revolutionary Movements Of Iraq*
Christopher Browning's *Ordinary Men: Reserve Police Batallion 101 and the Final Solution in Poland*
Edmund Burke's *Reflections on the Revolution in France*
William Cronon's *Nature's Metropolis: Chicago And The Great West*
Alfred W. Crosby's *The Columbian Exchange*
Hamid Dabashi's *Iran: A People Interrupted*
David Brion Davis's *The Problem of Slavery in the Age of Revolution*
Nathalie Zemon Davis's *The Return of Martin Guerre*
Jared Diamond's *Guns, Germs & Steel: the Fate of Human Societies*
Frank Dikotter's *Mao's Great Famine*
John W Dower's *War Without Mercy: Race And Power In The Pacific War*
W. E. B. Du Bois's *The Souls of Black Folk*
Richard J. Evans's *In Defence of History*
Lucien Febvre's *The Problem of Unbelief in the 16th Century*
Sheila Fitzpatrick's *Everyday Stalinism*

The Macat Library By Discipline

Eric Foner's *Reconstruction: America's Unfinished Revolution, 1863-1877*
Michel Foucault's *Discipline and Punish*
Michel Foucault's *History of Sexuality*
Francis Fukuyama's *The End of History and the Last Man*
John Lewis Gaddis's *We Now Know: Rethinking Cold War History*
Ernest Gellner's *Nations and Nationalism*
Eugene Genovese's *Roll, Jordan, Roll: The World the Slaves Made*
Carlo Ginzburg's *The Night Battles*
Daniel Goldhagen's *Hitler's Willing Executioners*
Jack Goldstone's *Revolution and Rebellion in the Early Modern World*
Antonio Gramsci's *The Prison Notebooks*
Alexander Hamilton, John Jay & James Madison's *The Federalist Papers*
Christopher Hill's *The World Turned Upside Down*
Carole Hillenbrand's *The Crusades: Islamic Perspectives*
Thomas Hobbes's *Leviathan*
Eric Hobsbawm's *The Age Of Revolution*
John A. Hobson's *Imperialism: A Study*
Albert Hourani's *History of the Arab Peoples*
Samuel P. Huntington's *The Clash of Civilizations and the Remaking of World Order*
C. L. R. James's *The Black Jacobins*
Tony Judt's *Postwar: A History of Europe Since 1945*
Ernst Kantorowicz's *The King's Two Bodies: A Study in Medieval Political Theology*
Paul Kennedy's *The Rise and Fall of the Great Powers*
Ian Kershaw's *The "Hitler Myth": Image and Reality in the Third Reich*
John Maynard Keynes's *The General Theory of Employment, Interest and Money*
Charles P. Kindleberger's *Manias, Panics and Crashes*
Martin Luther King Jr's *Why We Can't Wait*
Henry Kissinger's *World Order: Reflections on the Character of Nations and the Course of History*
Thomas Kuhn's *The Structure of Scientific Revolutions*
Georges Lefebvre's *The Coming of the French Revolution*
John Locke's *Two Treatises of Government*
Niccolò Machiavelli's *The Prince*
Thomas Robert Malthus's *An Essay on the Principle of Population*
Mahmood Mamdani's *Citizen and Subject: Contemporary Africa And The Legacy Of Late Colonialism*
Karl Marx's *Capital*
Stanley Milgram's *Obedience to Authority*
John Stuart Mill's *On Liberty*
Thomas Paine's *Common Sense*
Thomas Paine's *Rights of Man*
Geoffrey Parker's *Global Crisis: War, Climate Change and Catastrophe in the Seventeenth Century*
Jonathan Riley-Smith's *The First Crusade and the Idea of Crusading*
Jean-Jacques Rousseau's *The Social Contract*
Joan Wallach Scott's *Gender and the Politics of History*
Theda Skocpol's *States and Social Revolutions*
Adam Smith's *The Wealth of Nations*
Timothy Snyder's *Bloodlands: Europe Between Hitler and Stalin*
Sun Tzu's *The Art of War*
Keith Thomas's *Religion and the Decline of Magic*
Thucydides's *The History of the Peloponnesian War*
Frederick Jackson Turner's *The Significance of the Frontier in American History*
Odd Arne Westad's *The Global Cold War: Third World Interventions And The Making Of Our Times*

LITERATURE

Chinua Achebe's *An Image of Africa: Racism in Conrad's Heart of Darkness*
Roland Barthes's *Mythologies*
Homi K. Bhabha's *The Location of Culture*
Judith Butler's *Gender Trouble*
Simone De Beauvoir's *The Second Sex*
Ferdinand De Saussure's *Course in General Linguistics*
T. S. Eliot's *The Sacred Wood: Essays on Poetry and Criticism*
Zora Neale Huston's *Characteristics of Negro Expression*
Toni Morrison's *Playing in the Dark: Whiteness in the American Literary Imagination*
Edward Said's *Orientalism*
Gayatri Chakravorty Spivak's *Can the Subaltern Speak?*
Mary Wollstonecraft's *A Vindication of the Rights of Women*
Virginia Woolf's *A Room of One's Own*

PHILOSOPHY

Elizabeth Anscombe's *Modern Moral Philosophy*
Hannah Arendt's *The Human Condition*
Aristotle's *Metaphysics*
Aristotle's *Nicomachean Ethics*
Edmund Gettier's *Is Justified True Belief Knowledge?*
Georg Wilhelm Friedrich Hegel's *Phenomenology of Spirit*
David Hume's *Dialogues Concerning Natural Religion*
David Hume's *The Enquiry for Human Understanding*
Immanuel Kant's *Religion within the Boundaries of Mere Reason*
Immanuel Kant's *Critique of Pure Reason*
Søren Kierkegaard's *The Sickness Unto Death*
Søren Kierkegaard's *Fear and Trembling*
C. S. Lewis's *The Abolition of Man*
Alasdair MacIntyre's *After Virtue*
Marcus Aurelius's *Meditations*
Friedrich Nietzsche's *On the Genealogy of Morality*
Friedrich Nietzsche's *Beyond Good and Evil*
Plato's *Republic*
Plato's *Symposium*
Jean-Jacques Rousseau's *The Social Contract*
Gilbert Ryle's *The Concept of Mind*
Baruch Spinoza's *Ethics*
Sun Tzu's *The Art of War*
Ludwig Wittgenstein's *Philosophical Investigations*

POLITICS

Benedict Anderson's *Imagined Communities*
Aristotle's *Politics*
Bernard Bailyn's *The Ideological Origins of the American Revolution*
Edmund Burke's *Reflections on the Revolution in France*
John C. Calhoun's *A Disquisition on Government*
Ha-Joon Chang's *Kicking Away the Ladder*
Hamid Dabashi's *Iran: A People Interrupted*
Hamid Dabashi's *Theology of Discontent: The Ideological Foundation of the Islamic Revolution in Iran*
Robert Dahl's *Democracy and its Critics*
Robert Dahl's *Who Governs?*
David Brion Davis's *The Problem of Slavery in the Age of Revolution*

Alexis De Tocqueville's *Democracy in America*
James Ferguson's *The Anti-Politics Machine*
Frank Dikotter's *Mao's Great Famine*
Sheila Fitzpatrick's *Everyday Stalinism*
Eric Foner's *Reconstruction: America's Unfinished Revolution, 1863-1877*
Milton Friedman's *Capitalism and Freedom*
Francis Fukuyama's *The End of History and the Last Man*
John Lewis Gaddis's *We Now Know: Rethinking Cold War History*
Ernest Gellner's *Nations and Nationalism*
David Graeber's *Debt: the First 5000 Years*
Antonio Gramsci's *The Prison Notebooks*
Alexander Hamilton, John Jay & James Madison's *The Federalist Papers*
Friedrich Hayek's *The Road to Serfdom*
Christopher Hill's *The World Turned Upside Down*
Thomas Hobbes's *Leviathan*
John A. Hobson's *Imperialism: A Study*
Samuel P. Huntington's *The Clash of Civilizations and the Remaking of World Order*
Tony Judt's *Postwar: A History of Europe Since 1945*
David C. Kang's *China Rising: Peace, Power and Order in East Asia*
Paul Kennedy's *The Rise and Fall of Great Powers*
Robert Keohane's *After Hegemony*
Martin Luther King Jr.'s *Why We Can't Wait*
Henry Kissinger's *World Order: Reflections on the Character of Nations and the Course of History*
John Locke's *Two Treatises of Government*
Niccolò Machiavelli's *The Prince*
Thomas Robert Malthus's *An Essay on the Principle of Population*
Mahmood Mamdani's *Citizen and Subject: Contemporary Africa And The Legacy Of
Late Colonialism*
Karl Marx's *Capital*
John Stuart Mill's *On Liberty*
John Stuart Mill's *Utilitarianism*
Hans Morgenthau's *Politics Among Nations*
Thomas Paine's *Common Sense*
Thomas Paine's *Rights of Man*
Thomas Piketty's *Capital in the Twenty-First Century*
Robert D. Putman's *Bowling Alone*
John Rawls's *Theory of Justice*
Jean-Jacques Rousseau's *The Social Contract*
Theda Skocpol's *States and Social Revolutions*
Adam Smith's *The Wealth of Nations*
Sun Tzu's *The Art of War*
Henry David Thoreau's *Civil Disobedience*
Thucydides's *The History of the Peloponnesian War*
Kenneth Waltz's *Theory of International Politics*
Max Weber's *Politics as a Vocation*
Odd Arne Westad's *The Global Cold War: Third World Interventions And The Making Of Our Times*

POSTCOLONIAL STUDIES

Roland Barthes's *Mythologies*
Frantz Fanon's *Black Skin, White Masks*
Homi K. Bhabha's *The Location of Culture*
Gustavo Gutiérrez's *A Theology of Liberation*
Edward Said's *Orientalism*
Gayatri Chakravorty Spivak's *Can the Subaltern Speak?*

PSYCHOLOGY

Gordon Allport's *The Nature of Prejudice*
Alan Baddeley & Graham Hitch's *Aggression: A Social Learning Analysis*
Albert Bandura's *Aggression: A Social Learning Analysis*
Leon Festinger's *A Theory of Cognitive Dissonance*
Sigmund Freud's *The Interpretation of Dreams*
Betty Friedan's *The Feminine Mystique*
Michael R. Gottfredson & Travis Hirschi's *A General Theory of Crime*
Eric Hoffer's *The True Believer: Thoughts on the Nature of Mass Movements*
William James's *Principles of Psychology*
Elizabeth Loftus's *Eyewitness Testimony*
A. H. Maslow's *A Theory of Human Motivation*
Stanley Milgram's *Obedience to Authority*
Steven Pinker's *The Better Angels of Our Nature*
Oliver Sacks's *The Man Who Mistook His Wife For a Hat*
Richard Thaler & Cass Sunstein's *Nudge: Improving Decisions About Health, Wealth and Happiness*
Amos Tversky's *Judgment under Uncertainty: Heuristics and Biases*
Philip Zimbardo's *The Lucifer Effect*

SCIENCE

Rachel Carson's *Silent Spring*
William Cronon's *Nature's Metropolis: Chicago And The Great West*
Alfred W. Crosby's *The Columbian Exchange*
Charles Darwin's *On the Origin of Species*
Richard Dawkin's *The Selfish Gene*
Thomas Kuhn's *The Structure of Scientific Revolutions*
Geoffrey Parker's *Global Crisis: War, Climate Change and Catastrophe in the Seventeenth Century*
Mathis Wackernagel & William Rees's *Our Ecological Footprint*

SOCIOLOGY

Michelle Alexander's *The New Jim Crow: Mass Incarceration in the Age of Colorblindness*
Gordon Allport's *The Nature of Prejudice*
Albert Bandura's *Aggression: A Social Learning Analysis*
Hanna Batatu's *The Old Social Classes And The Revolutionary Movements Of Iraq*
Ha-Joon Chang's *Kicking Away the Ladder*
W. E. B. Du Bois's *The Souls of Black Folk*
Émile Durkheim's *On Suicide*
Frantz Fanon's *Black Skin, White Masks*
Frantz Fanon's *The Wretched of the Earth*
Eric Foner's *Reconstruction: America's Unfinished Revolution, 1863-1877*
Eugene Genovese's *Roll, Jordan, Roll: The World the Slaves Made*
Jack Goldstone's *Revolution and Rebellion in the Early Modern World*
Antonio Gramsci's *The Prison Notebooks*
Richard Herrnstein & Charles A Murray's *The Bell Curve: Intelligence and Class Structure in American Life*
Eric Hoffer's *The True Believer: Thoughts on the Nature of Mass Movements*
Jane Jacobs's *The Death and Life of Great American Cities*
Robert Lucas's *Why Doesn't Capital Flow from Rich to Poor Countries?*
Jay Macleod's *Ain't No Makin' It: Aspirations and Attainment in a Low Income Neighborhood*
Elaine May's *Homeward Bound: American Families in the Cold War Era*
Douglas McGregor's *The Human Side of Enterprise*
C. Wright Mills's *The Sociological Imagination*

Thomas Piketty's *Capital in the Twenty-First Century*
Robert D. Putman's *Bowling Alone*
David Riesman's *The Lonely Crowd: A Study of the Changing American Character*
Edward Said's *Orientalism*
Joan Wallach Scott's *Gender and the Politics of History*
Theda Skocpol's *States and Social Revolutions*
Max Weber's *The Protestant Ethic and the Spirit of Capitalism*

THEOLOGY

Augustine's *Confessions*
Benedict's *Rule of St Benedict*
Gustavo Gutiérrez's *A Theology of Liberation*
Carole Hillenbrand's *The Crusades: Islamic Perspectives*
David Hume's *Dialogues Concerning Natural Religion*
Immanuel Kant's *Religion within the Boundaries of Mere Reason*
Ernst Kantorowicz's *The King's Two Bodies: A Study in Medieval Political Theology*
Søren Kierkegaard's *The Sickness Unto Death*
C. S. Lewis's *The Abolition of Man*
Saba Mahmood's *The Politics of Piety: The Islamic Revival and the Feminist Subject*
Baruch Spinoza's *Ethics*
Keith Thomas's *Religion and the Decline of Magic*

COMING SOON

Chris Argyris's *The Individual and the Organisation*
Seyla Benhabib's *The Rights of Others*
Walter Benjamin's *The Work Of Art in the Age of Mechanical Reproduction*
John Berger's *Ways of Seeing*
Pierre Bourdieu's *Outline of a Theory of Practice*
Mary Douglas's *Purity and Danger*
Roland Dworkin's *Taking Rights Seriously*
James G. March's *Exploration and Exploitation in Organisational Learning*
Ikujiro Nonaka's *A Dynamic Theory of Organizational Knowledge Creation*
Griselda Pollock's *Vision and Difference*
Amartya Sen's *Inequality Re-Examined*
Susan Sontag's *On Photography*
Yasser Tabbaa's *The Transformation of Islamic Art*
Ludwig von Mises's *Theory of Money and Credit*

Macat Disciplines

Access the greatest ideas and thinkers across entire disciplines, including

AFRICANA STUDIES

Chinua Achebe's *An Image of Africa: Racism in Conrad's Heart of Darkness*

W. E. B. Du Bois's *The Souls of Black Folk*

Zora Neale Hurston's *Characteristics of Negro Expression*

Martin Luther King Jr.'s *Why We Can't Wait*

Toni Morrison's *Playing in the Dark: Whiteness in the American Literary Imagination*

Macat analyses are available from all good bookshops and libraries.

Access hundreds of analyses through one, multimedia tool.
Join free for one month **library.macat.com**

Macat Disciplines

Access the greatest ideas and thinkers across entire disciplines, including

FEMINISM, GENDER AND QUEER STUDIES

Simone De Beauvoir's
The Second Sex

Michel Foucault's
History of Sexuality

Betty Friedan's
The Feminine Mystique

Saba Mahmood's
*The Politics of Piety:
The Islamic Revival and
the Feminist Subject*

Joan Wallach Scott's
*Gender and the
Politics of History*

Mary Wollstonecraft's
*A Vindication of the
Rights of Woman*

Virginia Woolf's
A Room of One's Own

Judith Butler's
Gender Trouble

 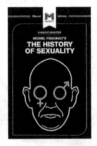  

Macat Disciplines

Access the greatest ideas and thinkers across entire disciplines, including

INEQUALITY

Ha-Joon Chang's, *Kicking Away the Ladder*

David Graeber's, *Debt: The First 5000 Years*

Robert E. Lucas's, *Why Doesn't Capital Flow from Rich To Poor Countries?*

Thomas Piketty's, *Capital in the Twenty-First Century*

Amartya Sen's, *Inequality Re-Examined*

Mahbub Ul Haq's, *Reflections on Human Development*

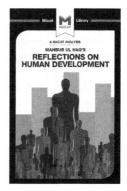

Macat analyses are available from all good bookshops and libraries.

Access hundreds of analyses through one, multimedia tool.
Join free for one month **library.macat.com**

Macat Disciplines

Access the greatest ideas and thinkers across entire disciplines, including

CRIMINOLOGY

Michelle Alexander's
*The New Jim Crow:
Mass Incarceration in the
Age of Colorblindness*

**Michael R. Gottfredson
& Travis Hirschi's**
A General Theory of Crime

Elizabeth Loftus's
Eyewitness Testimony

**Richard Herrnstein
& Charles A. Murray's**
*The Bell Curve: Intelligence and
Class Structure in American Life*

Jay Macleod's
*Ain't No Makin' It:
Aspirations and Attainment in a
Low-Income Neighborhood*

Philip Zimbardo's
The Lucifer Effect

Macat Disciplines

Access the greatest ideas and thinkers across entire disciplines, including

Postcolonial Studies

Roland Barthes's *Mythologies*
Frantz Fanon's *Black Skin, White Masks*
Homi K. Bhabha's *The Location of Culture*
Gustavo Gutiérrez's *A Theology of Liberation*
Edward Said's *Orientalism*
Gayatri Chakravorty Spivak's *Can the Subaltern Speak?*

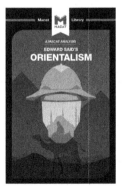

Macat analyses are available from all good bookshops and libraries.

Access hundreds of analyses through one, multimedia tool.
Join free for one month **library.macat.com**

Macat Disciplines

Access the greatest ideas and thinkers across entire disciplines, including

GLOBALIZATION

Arjun Appadurai's, *Modernity at Large: Cultural Dimensions of Globalisation*

James Ferguson's, *The Anti-Politics Machine*

Geert Hofstede's, *Culture's Consequences*

Amartya Sen's, *Development as Freedom*

Macat analyses are available from all good bookshops and libraries.

Access hundreds of analyses through one, multimedia tool.
Join free for one month **library.macat.com**

Macat Pairs

Analyse historical and modern issues from opposite sides of an argument. Pairs include:

HOW TO RUN AN ECONOMY

John Maynard Keynes's
The General Theory OF Employment, Interest and Money

Classical economics suggests that market economies are self-correcting in times of recession or depression, and tend toward full employment and output. But English economist John Maynard Keynes disagrees.

In his ground-breaking 1936 study *The General Theory*, Keynes argues that traditional economics has misunderstood the causes of unemployment. Employment is not determined by the price of labor; it is directly linked to demand. Keynes believes market economies are by nature unstable, and so require government intervention. Spurred on by the social catastrophe of the Great Depression of the 1930s, he sets out to revolutionize the way the world thinks

Milton Friedman's
The Role of Monetary Policy

Friedman's 1968 paper changed the course of economic theory. In just 17 pages, he demolished existing theory and outlined an effective alternate monetary policy designed to secure 'high employment, stable prices and rapid growth.'

Friedman demonstrated that monetary policy plays a vital role in broader economic stability and argued that economists got their monetary policy wrong in the 1950s and 1960s by misunderstanding the relationship between inflation and unemployment. Previous generations of economists had believed that governments could permanently decrease unemployment by permitting inflation—and vice versa. Friedman's most original contribution was to show that this supposed trade-off is an illusion that only works in the short term.

Macat Disciplines

Access the greatest ideas and thinkers across entire disciplines, including

THE FUTURE OF DEMOCRACY

Robert A. Dahl's, *Democracy and Its Critics*
Robert A. Dahl's, *Who Governs?*
Alexis De Toqueville's, *Democracy in America*
Niccolò Machiavelli's, *The Prince*
John Stuart Mill's, *On Liberty*
Robert D. Putnam's, *Bowling Alone*
Jean-Jacques Rousseau's, *The Social Contract*
Henry David Thoreau's, *Civil Disobedience*

Macat Disciplines

Access the greatest ideas and thinkers across entire disciplines, including

TOTALITARIANISM

Sheila Fitzpatrick's, *Everyday Stalinism*
Ian Kershaw's, *The "Hitler Myth"*
Timothy Snyder's, *Bloodlands*

Macat Pairs

Analyse historical and modern issues from opposite sides of an argument. Pairs include:

RACE AND IDENTITY

Zora Neale Hurston's
Characteristics of Negro Expression

Using material collected on anthropological expeditions to the South, Zora Neale Hurston explains how expression in African American culture in the early twentieth century departs from the art of white America. At the time, African American art was often criticized for copying white culture. For Hurston, this criticism misunderstood how art works. European tradition views art as something fixed. But Hurston describes a creative process that is alive, ever-changing, and largely improvisational. She maintains that African American art works through a process called 'mimicry'—where an imitated object or verbal pattern, for example, is reshaped and altered until it becomes something new, novel—and worthy of attention.

Frantz Fanon's
Black Skin, White Masks

Black Skin, White Masks offers a radical analysis of the psychological effects of colonization on the colonized.

Fanon witnessed the effects of colonization first hand both in his birthplace, Martinique, and again later in life when he worked as a psychiatrist in another French colony, Algeria. His text is uncompromising in form and argument. He dissects the dehumanizing effects of colonialism, arguing that it destroys the native sense of identity, forcing people to adapt to an alien set of values—including a core belief that they are inferior. This results in deep psychological trauma.

Fanon's work played a pivotal role in the civil rights movements of the 1960s.

Macat analyses are available from all good bookshops and libraries.

Access hundreds of analyses through one, multimedia tool.
Join free for one month **library.macat.com**

Macat Pairs

Analyse historical and modern issues from opposite sides of an argument. Pairs include:

INTERNATIONAL RELATIONS IN THE 21ST CENTURY

Samuel P. Huntington's
The Clash of Civilisations

In his highly influential 1996 book, Huntington offers a vision of a post-Cold War world in which conflict takes place not between competing ideologies but between cultures. The worst clash, he argues, will be between the Islamic world and the West: the West's arrogance and belief that its culture is a "gift" to the world will come into conflict with Islam's obstinacy and concern that its culture is under attack from a morally decadent "other."

Clash inspired much debate between different political schools of thought. But its greatest impact came in helping define American foreign policy in the wake of the 2001 terrorist attacks in New York and Washington.

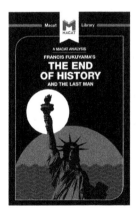

Francis Fukuyama's
The End of History and the Last Man

Published in 1992, *The End of History and the Last Man* argues that capitalist democracy is the final destination for all societies. Fukuyama believed democracy triumphed during the Cold War because it lacks the "fundamental contradictions" inherent in communism and satisfies our yearning for freedom and equality. Democracy therefore marks the endpoint in the evolution of ideology, and so the "end of history." There will still be "events," but no fundamental change in ideology.

Macat analyses are available from all good bookshops and libraries.

Access hundreds of analyses through one, multimedia tool.
Join free for one month **library.macat.com**

Macat Disciplines

*Access the greatest ideas and thinkers
across entire disciplines, including*

MAN AND THE ENVIRONMENT

The Brundtland Report's, *Our Common Future*
Rachel Carson's, *Silent Spring*
James Lovelock's, *Gaia: A New Look at Life on Earth*
Mathis Wackernagel & William Rees's, *Our Ecological Footprint*

Macat analyses are available from all good bookshops and libraries.

Access hundreds of analyses through one, multimedia tool.
Join free for one month **library.macat.com**

Macat Pairs

Analyse historical and modern issues from opposite sides of an argument. Pairs include:

ARE WE FUNDAMENTALLY GOOD - OR BAD?

Steven Pinker's
The Better Angels of Our Nature

Stephen Pinker's gloriously optimistic 2011 book argues that, despite humanity's biological tendency toward violence, we are, in fact, less violent today than ever before. To prove his case, Pinker lays out pages of detailed statistical evidence. For him, much of the credit for the decline goes to the eighteenth-century Enlightenment movement, whose ideas of liberty, tolerance, and respect for the value of human life filtered down through society and affected how people thought. That psychological change led to behavioral change—and overall we became more peaceful. Critics countered that humanity could never overcome the biological urge toward violence; others argued that Pinker's statistics were flawed.

Philip Zimbardo's
The Lucifer Effect

Some psychologists believe those who commit cruelty are innately evil. Zimbardo disagrees. In *The Lucifer Effect*, he argues that sometimes good people do evil things simply because of the situations they find themselves in, citing many historical examples to illustrate his point. Zimbardo details his 1971 Stanford prison experiment, where ordinary volunteers playing guards in a mock prison rapidly became abusive. But he also describes the tortures committed by US army personnel in Iraq's Abu Ghraib prison in 2003—and how he himself testified in defence of one of those guards. committed by US army personnel in Iraq's Abu Ghraib prison in 2003—and how he himself testified in defence of one of those guards.

Macat Pairs

*Analyse historical and modern issues
from opposite sides of an argument.
Pairs include:*

HOW WE RELATE TO EACH OTHER AND SOCIETY

Jean-Jacques Rousseau's
The Social Contract

Rousseau's famous work sets out the radical concept of the 'social contract': a give-and-take relationship between individual freedom and social order.

If people are free to do as they like, governed only by their own sense of justice, they are also vulnerable to chaos and violence. To avoid this, Rousseau proposes, they should agree to give up some freedom to benefit from the protection of social and political organization. But this deal is only just if societies are led by the collective needs and desires of the people, and able to control the private interests of individuals. For Rousseau, the only legitimate form of government is rule by the people.

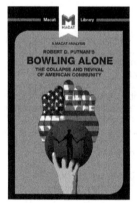

Robert D. Putnam's
Bowling Alone

In *Bowling Alone*, Robert Putnam argues that Americans have become disconnected from one another and from the institutions of their common life, and investigates the consequences of this change.

Looking at a range of indicators, from membership in formal organizations to the number of invitations being extended to informal dinner parties, Putnam demonstrates that Americans are interacting less and creating less "social capital" – with potentially disastrous implications for their society.

It would be difficult to overstate the impact of *Bowling Alone*, one of the most frequently cited social science publications of the last half-century.